Would you believe . . .

In Louisiana, a minister interrupts his Sunday sermon to answer his cell phone!

An engagement proposal at a romantic restaurant is interrupted by someone having a loud cell phone conversation at a nearby table!

A dentist spends forty-five minutes on his cell phone planning his next golf outing—while capping a tooth!

At the zoo, a man barely escapes a lion attack after trying to retrieve his cell phone from the animal's cage!

A woman at a job interview interrupts her prospective employer to answer her cell phone and proceeds to yell at her daughter for wanting to get her nose pierced!

At the local YMCA, a man is seen yakking away on his cell phone in the shower—with a towel on his head and the water running!

On a bus in Greece, a woman is too busy gabbing on her cell phone to notice that she got off the bus without her baby!

At a five-year-old's dance recital, a parent's musical ring tone goes off so loudly that it confuses the dancers, causing them to stop dancing and break down into tears!

CELL PHONE JERKS ARE EVERYWHERE . . .

WHAT ARE YOU GOING TO DO A

D1043479

THE JERK WITH THE CELL PHONE

THE JERK WITH THE

CELL PHONE

A Survival Guide for the Rest of Us

Barbara Pachter
and Susan Magee

MARLOWE & COMPANY
NEW YORK

THE JERK WITH THE CELL PHONE:
A Survival Guide for the Rest of Us
Copyright © 2004 by Barbara Pachter and Susan Magee

Published by
Marlowe & Company
An Imprint of Avalon Publishing Group Incorporated
245 West 17th Street • 11th Floor
New York, NY 10011-5300

AVALON
publishing group incorporated

Library of Congress Cataloging-in-Publication Data
Pachter, Barbara.
The jerk with the cell phone : a survival guide for the rest of us /
Barbara Pachter and Susan Pagee.
p. cm.
ISBN 1-56924-404-9
1. Cellular telephone—Humor. 2. Etiquette—Humor.
I. Magee, Susan. II. Title.
PN6231.C255P23 2004
395.5'3—dc22
2004015287

9 8 7 6 5 4 3 2 1

Designed by Pauline Neuwirth, Neuwirth & Associates, Inc.

Printed in the United States of America
Distributed by Publishers Group West

*To my son Jacob, my
pride and joy, who
never ceases to amaze me.*
—B.P.

*To my techno genius of a
wonderful husband, Dave.*
—S.M.

Contents

Author's Note

I always wanted to write books. The problem was, I needed some help. Susan Magee always wanted to become an etiquette expert, but she wasn't always very polite.

Then we met. I'm now a much better writer and Susan, thankfully, is much more polite. Of course I'm joking about Susan and the etiquette business. (She's still not polite, but at least she's very talented.)

Ten years and three books later Susan and I are still a team and, more importantly, good friends.

Though this book was created and written by both of us, it is my voice that appears on these pages.

We drew on many sources to create this book: the many people I have coached and met in my seminars, friends, co-workers, relatives, acquaintances, people we met in the grocery store line, newspaper and magazine stories, and Internet sites. Whenever I relate a story told to me or gleaned from another source, the quote or story appears in italics.

Barbara Pachter

Introduction

**Cell Phone Jerks Are
Taking Over the World!**

Okay, **cell phone** jerks probably aren't taking over the
world, but it seems that way sometimes, especially
when I hear stories like this one:

> *My husband invited his staff of six senior managers
> over to our home for dinner. One woman—my hus-
> band's most senior employee who was part of a nego-
> tiating group—arrived wearing her headset. I
> thought that was strange, to come into someone's
> home wearing a headset, but from the joking com-
> ments the others made when they saw her ("Look, it's
> grown roots! It won't come off until it's surgically
> removed . . ."), I gathered she was one of those people
> who is always on her cell phone.*
>
> *All through the cocktail hour, I waited for the joke to
> be over. As we sat down to dinner, I kept waiting for her
> to take off her headset—this was a somewhat formal*

dinner. Surely, I thought, she would unclip the phone from her sequined belt, turn it off, and put it away. Instead, she proceeded, not only to wear the headset throughout the evening, but to participate in a conference call during dinner!

She sat at the table and sometimes would talk to us, but at other times she would speak into her headset phone. I would suddenly hear, "Could you repeat that, please?" and I would start to repeat myself only to realize she wasn't talking to any of us.

We were all exchanging uncomfortable glances. I was very annoyed. I tried to give her the evil eye or my best cold stare but she didn't seem to notice. I kept hoping my husband would throw her out, but he didn't. After she finally hung up, during coffee and dessert, she admitted that she didn't really need to be on the call, but liked to hear the discussion. I wanted to throw a crème brûlée at her, but I didn't. But I was tempted!

I know you're thinking, *"But who would do that?"*

A cell phone jerk would.

(By the way, *jerk* is a great word. I highly recommend it. It's a fun, yet negative description without being mean; it's gender neutral, and even politically acceptable. Jerks are equal opportunity. Anyone can be a jerk, no matter your sex, age, race, religion, or income.)

But don't get me wrong. I don't think automatically that anyone with a cell phone is a jerk. I have a cell phone and I use it. If I'm driving and need help I can get it. If I'm walking down the street and I'm suddenly seized with the need to have Chinese food, I can order it on the spot. Peace of mind and hot lo mein. I love it.

What I don't love are cell phone jerks who do all sorts of amazingly rude things, like negotiate contracts during dinner parties.

Though I don't love this woman's rude behavior, I do love this story. In its insanity, it underscores some very key things about cell phone jerks—all briefly outlined below— that we need to know, if we're going to survive them.

CELL PHONE JERKS
ARE EVERYWHERE

We need to learn how to survive the jerks for the simple reason that there is nowhere for the Rest of Us (the non-cell phone jerks) to hide. You know you can't go to a friend's or co-worker's home, a restaurant, the movies, the theater, a national park, a classroom, take a train ride, play at a golf course, or even visit a public bathroom without being exposed (no pun intended) to a jerk on a cell phone.

And yet, the jerks can still surprise us by coming up with new and absurd places, like in showers and trees, to torment us. (See pages 82 and 89.) You will find some very funny and very extreme stories about where cell phone jerks do their incessant talking in the first part of this book.

Cell phone jerks are everywhere because they're multiplying faster than a rabbit on Viagra. With over 150 million cell phone users in the United States, the potential for jerk-like behavior is as vast as the sky in which satellites make it all possible.

And, sorry, you can't move to Canada. And no again for Europe. The Canadians and Europeans are as fed up and distressed as we are, except the Europeans have had even more time to get to this critical mass point of being *fed up*, since we're newer to the technology than they are.

Forget Asia and the Middle East.

In March 2004, more than 1.9 million people signed up for mobile phone services in India, making it one of the fastest-growing telecommunications markets in the world and taking the total number of their cell phone users to more than 33 million.

However, when it comes to cell phones, no country can match the cultural infiltration or the technological innovation of Japan—over 80 percent of the population uses a cell phone. Their cell phones are really sleek, mini computers now used to surf the web, transmit home movies, get directions, and even scan bar code information. And the next big thing for the Japanese: cell phones with TVs built-in (telly celly anyone?)

In many parts of the world, including Jerusalem, Bali, and Madrid, cell phones have been used by terrorists. A cell phone can be rigged to detonate a bomb from a safe distance. As if we needed more instruments of terror in the world.

The only exception to the growing use of cell phones on the planet is North Korea. In May 2004, the government banned cell phones because too much communication with the outside world is just not, in their opinion, a good idea. (One of the rare cases in which I'd actually defend the cell phone jerks.)

So, yes, except for North Korea, cell phone jerks really are everywhere and their equipment and capabilities are expanding rapidly. Cell phone jerks aren't just armed with phones anymore. Now they have cameras, videos, instant messaging, GPS capability, Internet access, and now, in Japan at least, television.

Now they have more ways to torment us by downloading songs from the Internet and forcing us to hear them, decorating their phones with nicer wallpaper than most people's apartments, and taking our pictures. Parents who have struggled to communicate with their teenagers now have a new challenge: translating instant-messaging lingo.

Do you know what this says?

NEtng 2 +?
or
H&K, tak caR

Of course you don't; you're still communicating the long, old-fashioned way. But to millions of people who use short text messaging, these hieroglyphics mean, "Anything to add?" and "Hugs and kisses, take care."

It does not end—the jerks are everywhere and their phones just keep getting more and more advanced.

CELL PHONE JERKS ARE GETTING WORSE

Since the late 1990s, people have been complaining, sometimes loudly, and sometimes responding with violence, to rude cell phone abusers.

Look online, look in the newspapers and magazines from five years ago, and look today: There have been, and still continue to be, countless articles, news stories, legislative actions, complaints, and yet nothing has changed. The cell phone jerks are still jerks, and because their numbers are growing, the problem is too.

Actually, forget the magazines and newspapers, look out the window of your car (but only for a second, please, I don't want to cause an accident), and you still see people driving at 70 mph with handheld cell phones. And even if someone is using hands free, the latest studies confirm what many of the Rest of Us have suspected all along—it's probably just not safe to drive and talk on a phone period. (See page 56 for the latest research results.)

Yet, drive badly and talk, the jerks do.

I do think that many cell phone jerks have reformed—

you'll find their stories in this book, too. In the grand scheme of things it just doesn't seem that way. But again, with thousands of new cell phone users signing up each day, there's always going to be a freshman class.

THE WORLD SEEMS TO BE FALLING APART THANKS TO RUDE JERKS

A friend said to me, "Barbara, you hear about rude people all the time. What's the deal with these jerks? Are we just a rude society?"

I think a lot of people fear that this is the truth. When you're at your kid's soccer game and there's a dad yelling into his cell phone *and* at his child from the sidelines, it's easy to think it's true. When there's a jerk in a movie theater making dinner plans during the movie, how could it not be so?

Just how rude are we? According to Public Agenda, a non-profit organization dedicated to unbiased public opinion research, very rude. The following statistics may shock you, or since you're reading this book, they may only confirm your deepest fears about what seems to be another disturbing trend—the "rude-truth" trend:

> ➤ Seventy-nine percent of Americans say a lack of respect and courtesy should be regarded as a serious national problem. (It is.)

> Sixty-two percent say that witnessing rude and disrespectful behavior bothers them a lot and 52 percent said the residue from such episodes lingers with them for some time afterward and can potentially lead non-jerks to become jerks. (I call this the "Kaboom Effect" and you'll read more about this later on.)

> Sixty-one percent believe a law banning cell phone use in public settings, such as movies and restaurants, would help curb rude behavior. (Yes, it would. Then we can go back to the good old days of complaining about those annoying candy wrappers and people who cough during movies.)

You may be thinking, case closed—we live in a rude world. It's getting worse. There's no hope. We're like Rome before the fall, only with better gadgets and hairstyles. Cell phone jerks are just rude people who should be banished to the island of etiquette misfits.

The rude-truth statistics above may accurately reflect our feelings of frustration, and even despair, about rudeness, but they really don't explain the reasons *why* people, including cell phone users, are rude. I have a lot to say about this topic and think I may surprise a few people in the course of this book.

THE CELL PHONE JERKS ARE OBLIVIOUS TO THE PAIN THEY CAUSE THE REST OF US

I know this may be hard to believe, especially after you read some of the incredible but true stories in this book—like people who will put their hands in hot chocolate sauce, public toilets, and even the cages of wild animals in order to retrieve a cell phone. Then there are the people who get celebrity performers so mad they have to stop their shows, and jerks who make constitutional claims who have obviously never even read the U.S. Constitution or who have watched so much *Law and Order*, they think they are lawyers.

But you'll also discover that many cell phone jerks aren't necessarily jerks on purpose.

Yes, you say, but how can someone not know that the number one complaint is that people yell on cell phones? How can they not know that it's not okay to answer the phone and talk during a performance or movie?

As you will discover, there are reasons. And, in dealing—or not dealing—with a cell phone jerk, it will help you to understand them. But, back to our gloriously rude story . . . After reading the dinner-party-gone-bad story, I hope you're also thinking, *"But why didn't someone tell her to hang up? Or, better yet, ask her to leave?"* And what you really want to know is, *"Did she get fired?"*

Let me say, if there was ever a cell phone jerk who deserved to be voted off an island, it was this Headset Henrietta.

Yet, no one did anything. (And, no, she wasn't fired over this incident.)

Anyone at that dinner party would have been within their rights to pull this woman aside and give her a reality check. But it was the host who really should have spoken to her and gotten that headset out of her hair. He was also her boss. He could have said, "You have been invited to my home for dinner. Your cell phone use is disrupting the whole evening. Please take off your headset and join us or you will need to take the phone call back at the office."

But he didn't. No one else did, either.

WHY THIS BOOK?

And this brings me to the heart of the reason why I'm writing this book: *People don't know how to confront the cell phone jerks to get them to hang up or lower their voices.*

Okay, yes, I do confess that a part of me wanted to write this book to join you in complaining and kvetching about cell phone jerks because sometimes they are funny and ridiculous in their jerky splendor. Some cell phone jerks inspire incredulity and even awe in the Rest of Us.

So, yes, I wanted to have some fun at the jerk's expense and Part One of this book is an exploration of where and how the jerks torment us. Though I offer suggestions for dealing with, or simply surviving, the jerks that you encounter throughout your day, Part One is really meant to cheer you up and help you laugh at some of the more ridiculous things they'll do and say.

Part Two of this book is about reclaiming the streets, the dining rooms, the restrooms, and the grocery store lines from the incessant and loud chatter of the cell phone jerks and the ring dinging of their phones at inappropriate moments. The cell phone jerks may be out of control, but the rest of us are in control—still, though I admit, some of us are hanging on by a frayed phone charger.

As I explain, we need to keep our wits—and even more importantly our tempers—in check. We need to ban together . . . actually, forget banning, we need a revolution—but a peaceful one. As you'll read later in this book, cell phone rage is sweeping our nation. Read these outrageous stories and you will see that more blood will be spilled, more fists will fly, more f-bombs hurled out into the air, unless the Rest of Us do something.

Yes, there are times when I'd like to take a hammer to the cell phone of the woman sitting next to me on the train to silence her phone conversation, which is related three decibels too high, about needing to have a diseased body part removed.

But, and this is a *big* but, as someone who has taught etiquette and assertiveness for many years, I know there's a better way than yelling in that woman's face, "Shut up! Please, just for five minutes stop yakking about your bad body parts!"

I know that grabbing her cell phone and throwing it out the window might feel good—really, really, good—for a few moments, but that high won't last. Eventually, I will have to own up to my own bad behavior and loss of control. Plus, who knows what bad behavior I'll get back from her? Besides, another jerk will just take her place and then another and another. So, cell phone bashing isn't the answer; it just doesn't work.

That's why we have to finally stop just complaining or losing our tempers and, when the time is right, take action against the cell phone jerks while there's still time.

No, you might say, I still want to revolt, gang up on the jerks, and stomp on their phones until they can't be used anymore.

Wait. Hear me out. . . . Throughout my career, I've heard lots of stories of people exhibiting bad, sometimes very bad, behavior, everything from jerks who clip their fingernails during meetings to a sales representative who dressed up as the Grim Reaper and went into a hospital's ICU on Halloween.

Yet, I've also seen some pretty tough cases turn around. Approached in the right way, I've seen jerks transformed into non-jerks. I've coached some of them, so I know they exist. This is why I advocate a peaceful revolution. Peaceful in this book means using an approach that I call polite and powerful behavior.

I know, I know, this isn't what you want to hear. But don't roll your eyes and make assumptions . . . like that I'm just too nice or that I'm just trying to turn you into a wimp. I'm not. Polite doesn't mean wimp. Polite and powerful is an incredibly effective way to deal with the jerks in your life. You'll see.

However, though I have hope, I'm not unrealistic. There are some hard cases out there. Can a man who answers his cell phone in church, proceeds to yell over the music, and then declare, just as the music stops, "I've got to get the hell out of here, I can't hear a damn thing," be saved?

Maybe not. But even so, there are coping strategies for the Rest of Us and there are actions we can take. If we can't beat him, we don't have to beat him up; there are constructive ways to vent our frustrations.

DON'T PUNCH 'EM, PEG 'EM

I talk a lot about Cell Phone Etiquette Guidelines, CPEGs for short, in this book. There are several, and they vary depending upon the where the cell phone jerk is, such as in a restaurant, on a train, or in a business meeting.

Throughout this book, a CPEG is the etiquette guide-line itself, like no yelling on cell phones or putting your phone on vibrate when you are a member of an audience. I talk about these the most since they involve the two biggest complaints the Rest of Us have about the jerks. (Why, you want to know, don't they know about these CPEGs? Don't worry, I have that explanation, too.)

When I refer to PEGing or PEGed, it means that you're taking action or have taken action against a cell phone jerk by either speaking up to him/her and reminding him/her of the CPEG, i.e. by saying, *"Please lower your voice."* Or, you hand the jerk a CPEG card—three of which you will find in the back of this book.

Do you remember when deaf people would approach you in the airport and hand you a card? That was the inspiration for the CPEG cards. They have a short and friendly statement asking the jerks in a nice way to alter how they are using their cell phones, such as, *"Could you please put your phone on vibrate? The ringing is disturbing us,"* without you actually having to say any-thing to the jerk.

Yes, it's a great idea, but before you hand out your cards to every cell phone jerk you find, please read all of the guidelines in the second part of this book. I don't want anyone getting punched or chased by a cell phone jerk.

ABOUT THE STORIES IN THIS BOOK

Unless otherwise noted that I found the story online or in a newspaper or magazine, the stories I share have been either told to me or e-mailed to me. For the most part, I don't use people's names or their titles, just their stories.

The bad news is that I don't have to make these cell phone horror stories up since there's no shortage of them. Some women are magnets for handsome men. I'm a magnet for bad behavior stories. People love regaling me with tales of the egregious, even twelve year olds. I asked one of my son's friends if he had any horror stories to share about someone using a cell phone inappropriately. He responded that one night he couldn't find his phone and he was in a panic. He looked everywhere and finally found it in his pants. I said, "Thanks, but that wasn't really a horror story." He replied, "It was horrible for me!"

I'm sure it was.

But the good news is that you, in your frustration and anger at these jerks, are not alone.

I DON'T HATE CELL PHONES

Please don't email me and accuse me of being a Luddite (someone who opposes technology). I'm NOT. As I already said, I love my phone. I love technology. I embrace it. I was one of the first people on my block to own a dishwasher with a pot scrubber cycle.

I love that the newest cell phones come equipped with GPS technology, you can simply dial 9-1-1 and the good guys can find you based on your cell phone location. (Now, if we can just get the Chinese food delivery people on this system, the world would be an even better place.)

In fact, I just read a story online in *Cell Phone News* about a bushwalker, who had been missing for two days in southern Tasmania, and was found when the crew on board the rescue helicopter spotted a light in heavy bush and were able to pinpoint the man's exact location. You guessed it, that light was the screen of the bushwalker's mobile phone. (That bushwalker certainly has a battery that can hold a charge.)

If you've ever been in the Home Depot searching among the lumber and paint for your significant other, been late to a meeting, or have wondered where your teenager was at eleven o'clock at night, you have to bow down to mobile technology. It's incredibly convenient and amazing.

But so are cell phone jerks—amazing, that is, in their obliviousness to how they impact the Rest of Us. My issue is not with the cell phone or its technology, it's with the person holding it, answering it, and screaming into it, when they're not being considerate of others.

It is because of those people and for the Rest of Us that I write this book.

EVERYWHERE A JERK, JERK

Technology . . . is a queer thing. It brings you

great gifts with one hand, and it stabs you in

the back with the other.

—CARRIE P. SNOW, COMEDIAN

Jerks on Trains, Planes, and Buses

"Would you mind talking to me for a while? I forgot my cell phone."

I don't know if this is good news or bad news, but New York City is now gonna set up a deal whereby you can use your cell phones on the subway. I don't know, to me nothing says success like getting a call on your cell phone on the D train.

—DAVID LETTERMAN

t's the end of a long day. You're tired, really tired. You had to run to make the 6:12 train. Now all you want to do is sit back and decompress in your seat, not think about anyone or anything and just relax.

But you didn't run fast enough; the quiet car is full.

Now you have to sit in *the other* car, a.k.a. the jerks-on-cell-phone car, and you know what that means—you'll hear inane things you don't want to hear from people you instantly dislike, like, "Hi, I'm on the train . . ." Or, worse yet, a woman screaming at her kids, a sleazy man discussing, in-depth, his love life (which is obviously a whole lot more interesting than yours), or some big shot planning his next meeting in Tokyo—as if you cared that he gets to fly first-class.

Yes, you are in a public space with strangers. Your behavior still matters. You know that. But why don't they? Why do these cell phone jerks seem to follow you around, giving all cell phone users a bad name?

Here they are, five of the commuting cell phone jerks we love to hate:

#1 LOVE-LIFE LOTHARIO

A man on the train was answering his personal ads on a cell phone directly behind me. I could hear every word. It was hard not to listen because he was speaking so loudly. I really wanted to do work but his conversations with these women were getting more annoying. He was giving the same speech to each one: "Wow, this is a surprise. You seem so interesting. I think we really have a lot in common. I'm so glad I called you because I almost didn't. You know how it is with these personal ads . . ."

Yes, now we all know.

I wanted to grab the phone from him and tell the woman on the other end of the line that he had just told the same spiel to the others and that he had not told the whole truth in his ad. He was going bald and those six-pack abs he was bragging about were more like a quart of warm beer.

I was single at that time and learned a lot. Beware of men answering personal ads on cell phones—they may be jerks.

#2 MINUTE-BY-MINUTE MARIO

How many times have you heard this earth-shattering conversation?

"Hi, it's me. It's about 6:15, I'm on the train. I should be there in about forty minutes."

Ten minutes later . . .

"Hi, it's me again. I'm still on the train. Making good time."

Ten minutes later . . .

"Hi, it's me. Still on the train. Shouldn't be too long now."

Ten minutes later . . .

"Hi, it's me. I should be there in a few minutes."

Ten minutes later . . .

"Yep, it's me. Just pulled in. See you soon . . ."

Wow. Thanks for sharing.

#3 NON-STOP NORA

There's a woman who rides my bus every morning and talks the whole time on her cell phone—for ninety minutes. Did I say the whole time? It's amazing that one person can talk so much and not pass out from lack of oxygen to the brain. I know more about this woman than I know about my own wife.

#4. LOOSE-LIPPED LARRY

Do we need to listen to yet one more young executive on the move plan his schedule or discuss his deals? I can't believe some of the things these people say. They even name names and give out phone numbers. Personally, I like hearing confidential information that I can use.

#5 ANNOYING AIRLINE ANNIE

A colleague of mine used to be the kind of cell phone jerk who, as soon as she boarded the plane, would frantically make phone calls as if she was leaving for outer space and not coming back for seven years.

However, one time she was on a plane, in first-class using her phone before the plane took off. She was talking negatively about the woman she had to work with the next day. You guessed it. The woman's boss was behind her and heard the whole story. (Gulp.)

Now she reads before take off.

Talk About Distraction . . .

I know a woman who left a ham (given by her employer as a Christmas gift) on her commuter train because she'd been talking on her cell phone. Imagine being the next person to sit in the seat? What's this? Why . . . it's a ham. This must be my lucky day!

But a ham is nothing compared to what a woman in Greece left on the bus . . . her baby. Yes, she was so busy talking on her cell phone that she got off the bus without her child. And as the Associated Press reported, it wasn't until she hung up the phone that she'd realized what she did. She then hopped in a taxi and chased the bus to the depot. The baby was fine. The mother, I'm sure, was the one who needed to recover.

RECLAIMING THE SILENT COMMUTE

A guy sat down next to me on the Metroliner in Washington and started making phone calls. I told him he could make one more call, but after that I'd start singing show tunes. He thought I was joking and kept on phoning. So I faced his right ear and started belting out, "If ever I would leave you, it wouldn't be in summer," which is from Camelot.

—JOE QUEENAN

The next time you're on the train and there's a cell phone jerk disrupting the peace, what can you do if you don't know any show tunes?

When I posted a section on my website called "Ask the Expert," I had many people writing in to discuss work issues with me. Many wrote about their experiences with cell phones jerks. Here are three examples of what disgruntled commuters told me (These letters let me feel like "Dear Abby" and also make me grateful that I can walk to my office.):

Dear Barbara,

On the train, this man is talking at the top of his lungs to a woman who is apparently his ex-girlfriend. Everyone is getting really fed up with him but no one is doing anything except rolling their eyes and shaking their heads because, I guess, no one knows what to do.

After about fifteen minutes of listening to him, I went, "Shhhh" really loudly. Then the jerk says into his phone, "Do you believe it? Someone is listening to my conversation and telling me to be quiet." It's like he's offended because I'm listening. I really wanted to strangle him then. A few minutes later, I snapped. I don't know what made me think of this but I started singing "99 Bottles of Beer on the Wall."

The guy next to me started singing and by the ninetieth bottle of beer, the whole car was singing and laughing and the jerk had fled. It was the single best moment of my life as train rider.

Sincerely,

Drowned Him Out in Delaware

Dear Drowned,

You are either really confident about your singing voice or you make friends fast.

I can't help but wonder what made you think of "99 Bottles of Beer on the Wall"? Was this train full of ninth-graders on their way to summer camp?

Actually, singing is not a bad strategy, especially if you can convince a few disgruntled commuters to join in with you. And given the turning tide against cell phone jerks, this shouldn't be too hard. (But, I have to ask, wouldn't you have felt like a jerk singing by yourself if no one else had joined in?)

I have heard from others who tell me that shushing can sometimes be an effective strategy, but it can't be a loud "shhhhhhh"—that's rude. Although, clearly in this instance, this jerk was out to be a jerk and wasn't going to quiet down. And for him to get any hint it may take about four or five loud issues of *"SHHHHHHHHHHHH-HH."* And that's *really* rude.

While I like the idea of collectively drowning out a cell phone jerk with a song, personally, "99 Bottles of Beer on the Wall" doesn't quite work for me. How about the *Sounds of Silence* or *The Cell Phone Revolt Anthem*, which I wrote with you in mind and have reprinted below. Copy it and give it out on your next train ride. Have fun with it!

Sincerely,

Barbara

The Cell Phone Revolt Anthem

(Sung to the tune of "On Top of Old Smokey")

Hey, you on the cell phone,
Did you think you're alone?
You're not and we've noticed
The drone of your tone.

Hey, you on the cell phone,
Are we invisible or what?
We don't want to hear your conversation,
No ifs, ands, or buts.

Hey, you on the cell phone,
You may think you're so cool
But we're right here behind you,
Calling you rude, a jerk, and a fool.

So hang up your cell phone,
Make your mom proud,
Show us you're a nice person
Who knows how to behave in a crowd

Alternate ending:

It's okay to have downtime
And not talk out loud.

Dear Barbara,

I'm fed up with all the complaining going on about cell phones! Let's get real. People are busy and time is short. The morning train commute is the perfect time to catch up. But every time I sit down, people are glaring at me as if I pulled a marching band out of my briefcase. I make a few quick phone calls to my office and I keep my voice down, so what's the harm?

Sincerely,

Busy in Boston

Dear Busy in Boston,

I hear you. You're busy. Your day is jammed packed and you are looking to save some time. But I also hear the people who say, "I am so tired of the endless loud chatter disturbing me."

So there you have it, the dilemma of the 22nd century: The desire to save time versus the desire to have some peace and quiet.

You said that you make a few quick calls and keep your voice down. If that is true, you probably aren't a cell phone jerk. Unless, of course, you are sitting in a "no-cell" car.

Yet, you also say that "people are glaring at you." Hmmmm . . . . If you're inspiring glares, your perception that you're just making a few quick calls and speaking in a normal voice may not be accurate. We're often not aware of our own behavior and how others view it. I call this the "It's Not Me, It's The Other Guy" Syndrome.

But, let's say you really aren't a jerk—you've been given the Good Cell Phone Stamp of Approval. The people around you may still glare because they've been subjected to so many loud jerks on trains they just can't take anymore.

So if you want to continue to use your phone on your morning commute, be sure to pay careful attention to your volume. If you really aren't a jerk, chances are the glares of doom will disappear once people realize that your cell phone use is not disturbing them.

Good luck with the glares!

Sincerely,

Barbara

Dear Barbara,

Please settle an argument between my girlfriend and me.

There's a woman on her bus who talks on her cell phone non-stop. She's one of these cell phone jerks who gives out a lot of personal information, including her home number. One day, my girlfriend had decided enough was enough and she copied down the woman's home number. When she got to work she called the woman's home number and left a message saying, "I'm on your bus every day and everyone completely hates you because you're so loud and what's wrong with you, you're so rude ..."

After that, the woman uses her cell phone a lot less and is much quieter and my girlfriend now says she's going to call every one who gives out their personal information. I don't think this is safe. My girlfriend says that her work phone appears as the main number and there are hundreds of people in her building, but I'm not convinced. Whose side are you on?

Sincerely,

Concerned, Yet Curious

Dear Concerned,

Why stop at a phone call? Your girlfriend could get a dark raincoat and a wig. She could duck in and out of alleys and follow this woman from the bus depot and find out where she works. Then she can bribe the receptionist for her name so that later she can send her a package with a dead fish wrapped in newspaper . . . Better yet, she could become a cell phone vigilante, complete with cape and blocked caller ID.

Okay, okay, I think I've made my point. This is not my recommended way of silencing a cell phone jerk. I have heard of people calling jerks who give out their cell or home numbers on trains and planes, but it's not something I recommend since it is so indirect and sneaky and then the jerk has your number.

I usually suggest more direct approaches, unless you are concerned for your safety. Though I agree with your girlfriend, I think the odds of the woman discovering her identity and exacting revenge are slim.

She could have said something to the woman along the lines of, "I'm sure you don't realize this, but we can all hear your conversation. Could you lower your voice, please," or, less directly, by giving her a CPEG card. (See "Give Out a CPEG Card," page 157, for guidelines on using your cards.)

Sincerely,

Barbara

The Five Golden Commuter CPEGs,
OR
Five Ways to Get More People to Like You

Okay, you're super busy and it really helps to get your daily conversation with mom done on your down time. But before you dial, consider the following:

1. Ask yourself on a scale of one to ten, "Do I have to make the call?" One being, "I'll call you when I get to the office," and ten being, "I think I'm bleeding." Chances are, unless it's a seven or higher, whatever you have to say can wait until you get to the office.

2. When you begin a cell phone conversation, remind yourself to speak in a quiet conversational voice. Simple? Yes, and amazingly effective. Remember that shouting won't help you hear the other person. If you start to shout, hang up; it's not the right time to have that conversation.

3. Put your phone on vibrate. Even gorillas and other primates have been trained to do this, so the I-don't-know-how excuse just doesn't cut it anymore. If you're truly hopeless, spring for one of the latest cell phones with an easy-to-find "etiquette setting"—that's what it's called in the manual, folks—right on the key pad. Mine is so easily activated and deactivated by pressing down on the * key that I press it just for kicks. (Kudos to the cell phone companies for realizing how much we need this.)

4. Don't discuss confidential or personal business that's just too personal—you never know who is listening and what they will do with the information. Words ending in "ogist," like proctologist, should be completely avoided.

5. Be aware of the facial expressions of the people around you. Are you getting the "Glare of Doom," or the "Laser Beam Stare of Hatred?" If you are, you may be a cell phone jerk. You may need to lower your voice.

The Cell Phone Jerk Test for Trains, Planes, and Buses

Tell the truth:

1. Have you gotten bruised or required stitches because you tripped stepping onto a train or bus? Why? Because you were talking and not looking where you were going?
2. Have you been told to lower your voice, had spitballs launched at you, or been kicked in the shin when on the cell phone?
3. Have you ever missed your bus or train because you were talking on your phone and lost track of time? (This is mostly inconveniencing yourself, but then others could be waiting for you and you would be a jerk to them.)
4. Have you ever missed your stop or left an important item—like your child—on the bus or train because you were so distracted by your conversation?
5. Has a steward on the plane had to remind you to turn off your phone, that the plane is taking off? Has he or she had to tell you twice? Did you still get your peanuts? Were they thrown at you?

If you answered "yes" to any of these questions, chances are you are exhibiting jerk-like behavior with your cell phone. Brush up on those CPEGS before someone sings show tunes, or worse, "99 Bottles of Beer," in your face.

Jerks at Work

For a list of all the ways technology has failed to improve the quality of life, please press three.

—ALICE KAHN, AUTHOR

Jerks with cell phones are all over the workplace. And why wouldn't they be? There are jerks in business with regular phones—like people who put you on hold and leave you there for twenty minutes—so, of course, there are jerks in business with their cell phones. And no doubt, some of them work with you.

Cell phone use has exploded in the workplace over the last ten years and the opportunity for misuse has expanded, too. When I tell the participants in my seminars that I am doing a cell phone survival guide, they laugh and say, "It's about time."

I think if employers really knew what they were

getting when they hire employees who are cell phone jerks, they would think twice before hiring them.

Here's my idea of a want ad that would appeal to a cell phone jerk looking for a job:

> **Wanted! A highly intelligent individual able to grasp complex concepts, like understanding that a "cube" has no ceiling or doors and that sound has been known to travel . . .**

My co-worker thinks her cube is made of steel and that the rest of us are deaf. She's one of those cell phone screamers. She thinks that if she uses her own phone, no one will know that she's making a lot of personal calls. It's more obvious now than ever. I think our whole area knows every detail of her personal life because we can all hear her on her cell.

> **. . . must be able to instill doubt, worry, and fear in our most valuable clients . . .**

I was on the phone in my car with a very difficult client. He said he needed to call me back, what was my number? I had just gotten my phone and I didn't know the number. I tried to fake him out by saying that I would call him back. Finally, I had to admit that I didn't know my number. He said, "Hmm . . . I wonder what other details you're forgetting."

➤ . . . must pretend to pay attention in meetings . . .

I was text messaging my co-worker who was sitting across from me in a meeting. I was telling her I was bored and complaining that our boss was droning on and on. My boss, who is of the old school, and doesn't like all this "new fangled technology," noticed that I wasn't paying attention. Just like my one of my old high school teachers he said, "Mr. Reilly, do you care to share what you're doing on your cell phone that's so much more interesting than your job?" Before I could recover and hit the "off" button, he grabbed the phone out of my hand and read it. Luckily, he doesn't know how to read the abbreviations in text messages.

➤ . . . and who will promise (with his or her fingers crossed) to be highly productive . . .

I was interviewing a woman for a position in our foreign-accounts division. She was well-qualified and was the best candidate I'd interviewed so far. It was looking very good for her. Then, I hear it—it's her cell phone ringing. I thought, "Well I've done that before, forgotten to turn off my cell phone. No big deal." But, then, she answered it. Okay, I thought, maybe she has a sick kid at home. Then she proceeds to have a conversation, a loud one, with one of her kids who obviously isn't sick and is, in fact, well-enough to want her nose pierced.

And that's not even the best part. After she threatens to kill her daughter for about two minutes, she hung up and said to me, "Oh, don't worry, I will never take personal phone calls once I'm working for you."

I just nodded and smiled but what I thought was, "Oh sure. And when I go home from work tonight a fairy will have painted my house."

> **. . . can occasionally be forgetful.**

I was running a meeting and a cell phone starts to ring and ring. We all turn to one of the women on our team and she's saying, "No, it's not mine. I turned off my phone. I'm positive."

Yet it was obvious that something was still ringing in her briefcase. It turns out she has two cell phones, one for work and one for home. She forgot to turn off her "home" cell phone.

All I could think was, why have two phones? One is enough to cause problems.

> **In return for your hard work, you will sometimes be treated well and occasionally highly valued . . .**

Our firm's higher-ups are always making these proclamations about how important we, the employees, are; how much our contributions are valued . . . I believed them until my first perform-ance review, which I waited six months to have. The managing partner makes a big deal out of for-warding his regular phone to his secretary so we won't be interrupted. But then, five minutes into it, his cell phone rang and he answered it—during my performance review. I couldn't believe it. He talked for about five minutes of the allotted time we had together. That made me feel special—NOT.

When the Unthinkable Happens to the Cell Phone Reachable

Some things really should be done in person . . .

When my daughter Kaley was born, she had complications and had to be put in the intensive care unit. I was at the hospital around-the-clock for a week. It was a stressful time. Imagine my surprise when my cell phone rang and it was my boss. He knew I was in the hospital with my wife. He knew that my newborn daughter was having health problems. And he fired me over my cell phone. I couldn't believe it. I said, "You couldn't have waited until I got back next week?" I think my boss just wanted to get it over with and because I had a cell phone he knew he could reach me.

WHO MOVED MY CELL PHONE: FOUR WAYS TO SILENCE CELL PHONE JERKS AT WORK

When it comes to the jerks at work, here's the good news for the Rest of Us. You *can* try the following so you feel better and less powerless against the jerks at work:

1. **Say something.** Work is one of the few places where you can usually say something to a cell phone jerk without worrying about getting punched or maimed (though there may be some exceptions.) Keep it simple and use a line like, "Can you please lower your voice? I can hear your conversation,"or "Would you please go outside, your conversation is disturbing the group,"or "Please don't let your phone ring. It's disturbing to others."

Yes, it really can be this easy. (But if the jerk is your boss you may want to consider your career options before you say something.) For more advice on successfully speaking up to a cell phone jerk (and why more people don't do this but should and why they often blow it when they do), see "Stop Complaining and *Do* Something," page 95.

2. Encourage your company to adopt a formal policy. Ask your boss or human resources department to de-jerk cell phone use in your company. Propose that a list of CPEGS be given out to employees, posted in meeting rooms, the company Intranet, and included it the company handbook. (See "Ten CPEGs for the Jerks at Work", page 31.) Many companies, including one of the largest pharmaceutical companies in the world, Johnson & Johnson, have established company policy prohibiting employees from driving while talking on their company paid cell phones. More and more, corporate executives realize the enormous liability they face if one of their employees should cause an accident while talking business on a cell phone. (See the box on page 30.)

3. Drop a not-so-subtle hint. Forget the cold stare or throat clearing. Most cell phone jerks are immune to our non-verbal signals—as I'll discuss later, they often don't know their behavior is affecting others. So, if you can't bring yourself to say something directly to the jerk, you can try the indirect way by leaving a copy of the "Ten CPEGs for the Jerks at Work," on page 31, in their mailbox or on their desk when they're not looking. I don't usually recommend this method because you run the risk that the jerk still won't get the message. They may think that every one has gotten CPEGs or it's just an office joke. It is usually best to be direct so there's no misunderstanding. And, of course, you could also be seen or discovered and then you'll feel like a jerk yourself (adding another ten steps back in your self-evolution) because you weren't just direct in the first place.

4. Hand the person a CPEG card. CPEG cards are a less-direct and less-intrusive way of saying something. (Though generally at work you are encouraged to speak directly to others.) We'll get to this in more detail on page 157. Please, please, please, don't do this until you've read the guidelines—I don't want you to become a jerk, too.

Cell Phones and Liability: The Bottom Line

* A Smith Barney stockbroker, who was driving and talking on his personal cell phone while on his way to a non-business related dinner, hit and killed a twenty-four-year-old motorcyclist, a father of two. Though he was using a personal phone on personal time, the broker claimed that he had been making cold calls for his work, which he was expected to do. Smith Barney eventually settled the suit for $500,000.

* A Virginia law firm was slapped with a $30 million wrongful death suit when an employee who was conducting business on a cell phone struck and killed a fifteen-year-old girl with her car. (Cell phone records showed that she was on the phone at the time of the accident, talking to a client.)

* The State of Hawaii agreed to pay $2.5 million as its share of liability for an accident involving a state employee who allegedly was talking on her cell phone when she hit a tourist from New Jersey. The victim sustained permanent brain damage.

DON'T PUNCH 'EM, PEG 'EM: TEN CPEGS FOR THE JERKS AT WORK

When using a cell phone for work or at work, **DO NOT:**

1. Choose the striptease melody, "La Cucaracha," "Beer, Beer, Beer" by the Clancy Brothers, theme songs from TV shows, especially *The A-Team* and *Bonanza*. And, no songs by any pop star young enough to be your child, like Britney or Justin.

2. Make sensitive or confidential business calls discussing private issues nor mention the names of clients in trains, restaurants, or any other public setting. If you're saying, "Can you keep a secret?" or "This isn't for public consumption yet," then why are you talking about it in public?

3. Act like a gearhead and use your handy AMPS or your PDA to surf the web or to send IM to your cell mates during meetings. Nor shall thou RX. If you understand these abbreviations and lingo, you know who you are.

4. Wear any more than one wireless device on your body. You can't be professional if you seem like you're plugged into a wall somewhere.

5. Have personal- or business-related cell phone conversations in the bathroom at work—even if you've checked for feet. (You never know who may walk in.)

6. Walk and cell phone talk in the hallways or elevators. You need to meet and greet people, not shut them out or walk into walls. If you're walking with a headset, you will not only be rude, you'll look like you're talking to yourself—not a good idea at work.

7. Sit down for a meeting and put your cell phone on the table next to your Palm Pilot, your PDA, and your laptop—this screams, "I'm a cell phone jerk!" Turn it off and put it away. (You'll survive.) If you absolutely must keep your phone on (because of an emergency), put it on vibrate. Excuse yourself and don't answer until you're in a private place.

8. Answer your cell phone when you're having a discussion with a co-worker. Doing so means that you're saying, "Sorry, but this other person is way more important than you." Who likes to be ignored? No one.

9. Make personal calls from your cell phone from your cube, especially if you've just broken up with your boyfriend or girlfriend or you otherwise need a box of tissues to get through the call.

10. Cell yell. Please DO NOT speak loudly.

Cell Phone Jerk Sniglets:

Words and Phrases That Aren't in the Dictionary, But Should Be

BUZZERK: The panic people experience when they can't get their cell phone out of their pocket in time.

CPEG: Stands for Cell Phone Etiquette Guidelines, which the jerks need to start following.

CELLBLIVION: A failure to note the hostile body language of others around you.

CELLBOTOMY: Not having any common sense when you use your cell phone.

CELLCHOSIS: The belief that if you leave home without your cell phone, you will die.

CELL ENVY: The constant need to upgrade your cell phone.

CELLINANITY: Having meaningless conversations for the heck of it.

CELLFOOLERY: Pretending to speak on a cell phone in order to appear important to others.

CELLULUS INTERRUPTUS: When someone answers a cell phone during sex.

CELLSYMPHONY: The sound of musical ring tones going off during a public performance.

CELLULUSIONAL: The belief that you can drive safely while holding a cup of coffee and using your cell phone at the same time.

CELL YELL: The irrational tendency of cell phone users to speak loudly or even scream into their phones in the mistaken belief that doing so will make it easier for them to hear better.

CYCLECELLCHOSIS: The delusion that if you ride a bicycle in traffic and talk on a cell phone you are suddenly not made of flesh and blood, but rock and steel.

DIVORCELL: Legal grounds for divorce if a partner is caught cheating via his or her cell phone.

HELTER SKELTER CELLULAR: The public display of twenty people reaching into their coats when a cell phone rings.

KABOOM EFFECT: Suddenly exploding at a cell phone jerk one day because you can't take it anymore.

MOBILEBOTOMY: Not remembering how you got home because you were talking on your cell phone.

RINGUS STINGUS: The embarrassment you feel when your phone goes off in an audience and every one stops and looks at you with the Glare of Doom.

Jerks in the Audience

You go to a concert or to the theater and there are signs and posters in seven languages saying, *"Please turn the ringer of your cell phone or pager off"* or, *"Please, cell phones in the lobby only."* (I think I even saw one in Latin once that read *"Cellula non grata."*) You go to the movies and during the coming attractions a dancing popcorn box reminds the audience to "turn off your cells phones."

Yet, there's always a cell phone jerk with a cell phone ringing and I'd swear, he or she is always in the seat behind me.

In my more generous moments, I can understand someone forgetting to turn off his or her cell phone. I have done it. We all have. This is why it is so important to have an actual human being to remind people before the show to turn off their phones or put them on vibrate. People don't always read the signs or programs. I know that sounds strange since you are reading this book, but, trust me, it's true.

But what I really don't understand is *why* people go on to answer their phone and *why* they proceed to have a conversation while in an audience.

People go to a show to be entertained or to experience the event. This is not the time to schedule appointments, confirm dinner reservations, or chitchat with your mother. I'm simply stunned that people have to be told not to talk on a phone when they are an audience member. But—big sigh—they do.

AWARD-WINNING
CELL PHONE JERK SILENCERS

But let's not focus on the negative. Let's focus on the heroes out there, the well-known and not so well-known, who are working to restore silence in the audience for the betterment of the Rest of Us.

In fact, let me give out some awards. Here they are, in no particular order—our heroes.

The Duct Tape Award

For an actor who handled a cell phone jerk from the stage, the nominees are:

1. Kevin Spacey, who stopped mid-scene and quipped, "Tell them you're busy."
2. Laurence Fishburne, who interrupted his scene and yelled, "Will you turn off that f—ing phone, please?"

3. Brian Dennehy, who calmly said to the audience member whose cell phone was ringing, "Alright, let's stop. We'll wait while you find your phone and turn it off, have your conversation, whatever it is, but we'll just wait."

And the award goes to Kevin Spacey. Though the victims of cell phone abuse would probably vote for Laurence Fishburne, who got a standing ovation from the audience, as the mother of a 13-year-old, I just can't condone dropping the f-bomb in public.

Humor is often a good strategy when dealing with a cell phone jerk in public. You're not rude, yet the jerk usually gets the point that he or she is a jerk. Everyone wins.

The Silent Scream Statue

For a talk show host's handling of cell phone interruptions, the nominees are:

1. David Letterman, for announcing that any cell phones that go off during the taping will be smashed with a hammer.

2. Jay Leno, who reportedly took a woman's cell phone out of her hand when it rang during his monologue. He answered the woman's phone, saying, "This is Jay Leno. I'm in the middle of my monologue right now, so is there a message I can take?"

3. Ellen DeGeneres, for once having a section on her website entitled, "Audience Etiquette" that reads:

Please, no coughing.

I cannot supply cough drops at my shows. I wish I could, but it's not in the budget. However, feel free to bring your own cough suppressants, but be sure to unwrap them before the show. Crinkling is just as annoying as coughing.

Turn 'em off.

Before the show, double-check and make sure you've turned off your cell phones, pagers, and espresso machines.

And, of course . . .

Don't forget to enjoy the show!

And the statue goes to Ellen DeGeneres for not only tackling cell phones, but coughing jerks and candy wrapper jerks (subjects for my next two books). Although, kudos to Jay Leno for his forthright and direct approach.

The Albert Einstein Prize

For technological innovation that we wish we had *now*, the nominees are:

1. The researchers at the Royal College of Art in London, for inventing the "molar mobile"—the world's first tooth phone. (No, this isn't a joke.) It works via a tiny wireless embedded in your back molar that picks up radio waves. A magnet then converts incoming signals into sound waves, which vibrate from the tooth, up the jawbone, and to your inner ear.

2. Zetron, a company based in Redmond, Washington, for making a cell phone detector. When this gadget detects a signal within a ninety-foot radius, it lights up a message on a display unit and issues the warning, "Please turn your cell phone off."

3. Q-Zone, for making an automatic courtesy system for mobile phones that creates quiet zones in public places, like movie theaters and restaurants. When a mobile phone enters a designated quiet zone, its ring volume changes—switching to vibrate or diverting callers to voicemail.

And the prize goes to Q-Zone. This gets my vote because it actually alters the ring for you rather than just reminds or warns the caller to do it. But because Q-Zone is based on Bluetooth (wireless technology that enables connection between devices), it will not be widely available until more phones are using Bluetooth technology. (For more information, please visit: www.bluelinx.com.)

A Lifetime Supply of Popcorn with Butter

For a creative idea submitted to the management by a disgruntled moviegoer, the nominees are:

1. Brent, who suggested, "Put a giant metal bird claw in the ceiling. If someone's cell phone rings or anyone talks on one, the claw will swoop down and carry the person away. I call my invention the Eagle's Claw of Justice."

2. Stacy, who wrote, "Hire bouncers with big muscles just like they do in night clubs."

3. Hank, who said, "If your phone rings and you answer it, you have to buy everyone in the theater Goobers or Raisinettes. If you threaten to sue, you have to throw in a soft pretzel."

And the popcorn goes to Hank. Who wouldn't love a free box of Raisinettes? Though I think this would be a tough one to enforce. The most realistic way to handle a cell phone jerk in the audience is to quash the urge to scream and throw things and politely say, "We can hear your conversation. Please take your call outside." If they don't, you can go get the manager. You're not going to enjoy the movie anyway, so you might as well take action.

The Jerk Who Made
the Five Year Olds Cry

My five-year-old daughter's dance class was having a recital. For the finale, the girls were dressed like animals and singing "Old MacDonald." Right in the middle of their adorable performance, a man's cell phone went off and it was loud. Hearing the musical cell phone interruption, the girls got confused and stopped. People in the audience laughed. Then it was like lightening had struck in the barnyard. The chicken cried, the duck ran off the stage, and the horse took off her head and shouted, "What's going on here?" I think you have to be an inconsiderate person to upset a group of five year olds.

I agree.

Jerks in Restaurants

Five years ago, when I was in London on my honeymoon, I had a cell phone revelation.

We were with British friends in a restaurant. The topic of cell phones—which were already more commonplace there—came up and I went ballistic, politely of course. I started talking about how terrible it is that people talk in restaurants and bars on their phones. On and on I went—how rude it is, how disturbing to others . . .

My friend let me rant for a while and then, using her best British sense of understatement, said, "Do you see that woman next to us? She's been on her cell phone the whole time that we've been here. And you didn't even know it because she wasn't disturbing us. What do you think now?"

Ouch.

That experience made me rethink my position on cell phones in restaurants. After all, as a frequent business traveler who dined alone, there were times when I appreciated, and occasionally still do, using a cell phone when I'm dining alone.

Don't get me wrong. I don't use my cell phone because I feel uncomfortable dining alone—I enjoy the peace and quiet of my own company sometimes—and I would encourage you not to feel like you need to use your phone if you're alone simply because you are alone. But to be fair, the other side of this issue is that we usually go to restaurants to eat in the company of others. We have conversations. So, if you can talk to your friend across the table, why can't I, if I am alone, talk to my friend on my cell phone?

So, I'm going to say something you probably don't expect: though I would hope you don't feel compelled to use your cell phone when dining alone, I think it's okay for a diner to use a cell phone in a restaurant.

You did hear me correctly. I did just say you can use your phone in a restaurant, but, there is a but here. And it is a *big but* because the following CPEGs must be met:

> You are alone. (We know it's not because you have no friends—you could be traveling for business or just by yourself that night.) It's rude to speak on your cell phone, unless it's an emergency, when you're with another person or people, especially when dining.
> Your phone is set to vibrate.
> You speak in a normal conversational voice that does not make other people notice you.

> You don't interfere with the waiter servicing your table, i.e. you don't wave him or her away for fifteen minutes while you catch up with your girlfriend.

Absolutely, positively, no exceptions.

Okay, just one exception . . . I recently heard a story on National Public Radio about a group of wives of Marines stationed in Iraq. If a cell phone rings when these women are out together they all race to grab their phones, as the call would very possibly be one of their husbands calling—and they don't want to miss a call, which is, of course, completely understandable.

Military families are the only exception to the rules above, except if you're in the midst of a real emergency, i.e. the restaurant is on fire or you have to get to the hospital.

But as for the rest of the cell phone users out there . . . The problem is that there seems to be only a handful who even come close to following the four CPEGs outlined above. Unfortunately, it appears that the majority of people don't follow guidelines, as these types of cell phone jerks so rudely remind us:

> **Jerks on Dates:** *My husband and I were out for a romantic Valentine's Day. The man at the next table talked on his cell phone for fifteen minutes while his date just stared at him. Now that's love.*

> **Jerks Who Cell Yell:** *The woman at the next table was very considerate to her dining companions. When her cell phone rang, she turned away from them and proceeded to blare her conversation into our faces instead.*

> **Jerks Who Power Lunch:** *Four people sit around a table in a crowded upscale Italian restaurant, each with his ear stuck to a cell phone. The sound of four separate animated conversations fills the air. The server, busily attending to other tables, returns time and again to take the foursome's dinner order, to no avail. Finally, she jots a note that she rips from her order pad and places in the center of the table: "Call me when you're ready to order."*
> SOURCE: Nancy Hobbs, *The Salt Lake City Tribune.*

> **Jerks Who Are the Waiters:** *A friend of mine, an extensive international traveler, swears that when dining in Italy, you have to interrupt your waiter to get him to take your order because so many of them are talking on cell phones.*

I personally volunteer to go to Venice and check this out. I'll get back to you on this one.

When the
Shoulder Wedge Fails

This four-star *hotel has a chocolate and dessert buffet. I saw a man talking on the tiniest cell phone I have ever seen, while dipping a strawberry into hot chocolate sauce. Because the phone was so small, he couldn't keep it tucked into his shoulder. When his tiny phone fell into the hot chocolate sauce the chef had to stop him from putting his hand into the fondue pot. The man got all upset and said, "But it's a very important call." The chef said, "Sir, I'm sorry but I can't allow you to burn yourself."*

"Is that your 'God Bless America' or mine?"

THE RESTAURANT REVOLT

"Cell phone jerks are very rude to us," a restaurant server told me. "They often don't say hello. They might sit there for fifteen minutes talking on the phone before even looking at a menu. And when you go up to them, they seem upset that you are interrupting their call."

A woman I know who worked in a restaurant told me this cautionary tale:

You should be careful about how you treat the people who handle your food. I once saw one of the waiters, who was fed up with his rude cell phone customer, pick up a piece of chicken off a plate he was about to serve, and he pretended it was a phone—he was holding it to his ear and mouth. I also don't recommend eating the pickle spears on the garnish if you've been talking on your cell phone a lot either.

Yikes. Though I would never condone the illicit use of a pickle, I can certainly understand the hurt and frustration that someone trying to wait on a cell phone jerk would feel. I've said it before and I'll say it again: No one likes to be ignored.

But rather than exacting revenge upon a chicken leg, I think that managers and owners of restaurants need to continue posting polite signs explaining their cell phone policy, like no cell phones in the dining room or switch phones to vibrate. Though some may worry that they'll lose business by angering the cell phone jerks, the Rest of Us need to remind the owners and managers that our business matters, too. They can take an example from the following trailblazers:

> ➤ Ed Moose, who owns the famous San Francisco eatery Moose's, was one of the early pioneers of cell phone free dining policy. He said that when he saw one patron at one end of the bar use a cell

phone to call a friend at the other end, he knew it was time to act.

➤ Other restaurants now have a cell phone lounge or special section just for cell phone users. So, it has come to pass that smokers and cell phone users are often in the bar or out front together getting a fix.

➤ There is even a small custard stand on the way to the Atlantic City that had put up a small hand-written sign (smeared with chocolate sauce, of course) that says, "*Please do not speak on your cell phone when giving your order. We want to be able service you correctly.*"

This informal policy approach often works and it has stopped some of the annoying cell phone use. After all, we are a society of law and most of us are law-abiding citizens who will follow posted guidelines.

Forget the Fly in the Soup:

Helpful Hints for a Cell Phone Free Dinner

As a patron, if there is no sign or the policy isn't working, you can try the following steps:

1. Ask the host/hostess or manager to intervene. If he or she says, "Sorry, we don't have a policy," or "I can't do that," don't yell, "That's crazy!" Instead, you can reply, "I don't understand your reluctance. Many restaurants have policies. We love your food, but when you don't have a cell phone policy, it makes it difficult for us to come here and enjoy our meal." (Hint: We'll take our business elsewhere.)

2. Resist the urge to throw a bread basket, especially if the rolls are hot, and politely say something to the cell phone jerk, like, "Could you please lower your voice, we're hearing your whole conversation."

3. A less intrusive way to get your point across—simply hand the cell phone jerk a CPEG card, which you can find at the back of this book. (Actually, I think restaurants should keep a large stack of these handy so waiters can hand them out.)

4. As a last resort ask to be moved. However, if it's a restaurant with no policy or one that doesn't enforce its policy, you may be moving to the vicinity of yet another cell phone jerk. Look before you leap.

CREATIVE COMEBACKS FOR CELL PHONE JERKS IN RESTAURANTS

I know, I know . . . The cell phone jerks are going to say that I said it's okay to use cell phones. (Isn't this how politicians get into trouble?) Not only will they say that I said it's okay, they may even claim a constitutional right. So, here's what I would suggest as a few creative comebacks:

Cell Phone Jerk: But Barbara said it's okay.
Comeback: Read my lips . . . and the CPEGs on page 45. It's not okay if you're annoying other people.

Cell Phone Jerk: It's my First Amendment right to use my cell phone.
Comeback: Please! The framers of the United States Constitution did not intend for free speech to mean that others had to hear about your Aunt Betty's ulcer or the details of your divorce over a shrimp cocktail and chicken marsala.

Cell Phone Jerk: If my wife doesn't mind that I'm speaking on the phone, why should you?
Comeback: Are you sure she doesn't mind? Let's wake her up and ask her.

Cell Phone Jerk: The technology was made to be used.
Comeback: So were wind machines. We'll bring one right over to your table.

Cell Phone Jerk: But I absolutely must be reachable.
Comeback: Ma'am, I assure you, if the transplant team, the Pope, or the President of the United States calls, we'll be sure to put the call through.

HALL OF SHAME

The One Conversation
You Don't Want to Overhear
if You're Eating Mexican

A woman was on her cell phone talking to, I assume, another mother (I don't know that for sure but who else would be interested?) about her baby's pooping issues. She was going on and on about the color (green) and the frequency (a lot) and then my guacamole and chips arrived.

5

Jerks Who Drive

It's so frustrating . . . you're cruising along, listening to the radio, and you look in your rear view mirror—and WHAM, there he is. The cell phone talker going 75 mph and pasted to your bumper. It's not a pretty site.

admit it. I've done it. I've been the jerk on a cell phone while driving. Luckily, I didn't hurt anyone or dent anything, but while dialing, I have swerved on a highway. If someone had been right next to me, I would have scared them, and maybe even inspired a road rage incident.

I drove and dialed for the same reason that mostly every one else does—I was trying to save time. I was using my drive time as a chance to catch up.

But my wake-up call came (pun intended) when I realized that though I might save a few minutes, if I had caused an accident that call would have cost me a whole lot more than a few minutes. I am now one of those people who pulls over to make a call or (gasp!) I wait until I get to where I'm going. I know, I know, call me old fashioned.

Unfortunately, the cell phone jerks drive badly but never answer the wake-up call (they're too busy chatting to hear the ring), and they continue to drive and talk. They either don't realize they're driving unsafely or they don't think that anything bad will happen to them or because of them. And they are definitely not aware that they could be scaring others. In other words, as long as no glass or bones have been broken the jerks are saying: "What are you people complaining about?"

cell Phone Jerks Who Drive

Here are five good reasons why cell phone jerks who drive need to wake up and smell the strawberry rearview mirror deodorizer:

1. They drive with their elbows and knees.

The only thing that has ever shocked me more than seeing people talking on cell phones and driving with their elbows or knees was the guy I saw one morning on the New Jersey Turnpike driving with his elbows because he was talking on his phone and playing a banjo.

2. They act like we're the ones who are insane.

I was stopped in traffic and a guy talking on a cell phone rear-ended me. He gets out of his car screaming, "Why did you stop? You crazy @%t#&!" I didn't say a word. I just pointed at the red octagon with the word "stop" on it.

3. They present us with philosophical dilemmas that we don't want to have.

I'm in the middle lane on the freeway right outside of LA. I look in my rearview mirror and there's a kid on a cell phone in a rusty Camero riding my bumper. So I think, I'll just move into the left lane and let him pass me. But in the left lane there's a woman in a giant SUV having a cell phone conversation and swatting at her kids in the back-

seat. Okay, so the right lane it is. Wrong. I look over and there's a grandmother sitting in a car on a cell phone barely breaking the speed limit. I'm surrounded. So I have to ask myself, who am I most afraid of?

4. They make us drive like jerks.

I can't tell you how many times, I've had to make a break for the left lane and go 80 mph just to get away from the jerks on their cell phones. I wonder if the cop would believe me.

5. They don't learn from their mistakes.

My husband is a cop. He can't stand cell phone drivers because they're dangerous. Our town is one of the few in the country that actually has a law banning handheld cell phones. He pulled this woman over once and she tried to get out of getting a ticket by claiming that she was talking to herself. Another time, he pulled this guy over and he stayed on his cell phone. He said, "Why should I hang up if I'm pulled over?"

Two-fisted Drive

The International Herald Tribune reported that Scottish police stopped a man who they said was driving erratically on a busy street in Haddington. The driver, the owner of four local pubs, was not drunk. But he was using not one, but two, mobile phones while driving.

It's a Small World
(But I wouldn't want to pay the cell phone bill)

And speaking of international driving issues, take a look at these facts:

More than forty countries around the world—from Austria to Zimbabwe—currently restrict or ban cell phone use while on the road.

In Britain, using handheld cell phones while driving is now a criminal offense. Insurance companies will not reimburse drivers accidents caused by cell phones.

In Europe, there are restrictions against handheld cell phones in France, Germany, Spain, Italy, the Netherlands, Norway, Sweden, Denmark, Finland, and Poland.

A recent study by the phone company Telstra shows that one in five motorists in Australia take their eyes off the road to send text messages while driving.

IS IT EVER OKAY?

In my unpopular opinion, there are only three without-a-doubt allowable situations in which it's okay to use your cell phone in a moving car when you're the driver.

Here they are:

1. You're stuck in a traffic jam and not going any-where. (But when you start moving it's time to stop the call if it's a handheld phone.)
2. You're truly in an emergency situation, such as you've witnessed an accident or a kidnapping and you're following the car.
3. You are the kidnap victim.

See, I'm not unreasonable.

WHAT CAN THE REST OF US DO ABOUT JERKS WHO DRIVE UNSAFELY?

First of all, I don't recommend catching up to a driver going 60 mph on the highway, rolling down your window, and politely asking him to put his phone away as you try to control your car. Don't do this. It's not a pretty picture and it's unsafe.

Many of the suggestions I share give you polite and pow-erful ways to confront the jerk. (If you keep hoping that I'll give up this peaceful approach . . . keep hoping.)

But alas, polite and powerful just won't work for the cell phone jerk in a car.

So we've got to hope the law will act and act quickly. Remember when wearing a seatbelt was optional? And how your parents just threw you in the backseat and drove away? Now seat belts and car seats for children are the law.

You *can* encourage lawmakers to make laws to change dangerous driving behavior. Write your legislators. We always assume someone else is going to write those "Dear Congresswoman" letters. And today, you don't even have to write a letter and put a stamp on it, you can simply visit your state legislator's website and send an e-mail. It's easy.

(See "Jerks Who Drive and the Law," page 70.)

FOUR MORE WAYS TO DEAL WITH THE JERKS WHO DRIVE

While you're waiting for the legislative process to catch up to what the Rest of Us have already caught on to, that driving while yakking isn't safe, you can empower yourself. Here are my other suggestions:

1. Get out the way. I know this may be hard for some of you, but my policy for dealing with car phone jerks is *get out of their way fast.* Sometimes, when it comes to surviving the jerks we need to do just that, survive. So my policy is, "Let it go . . . and change lanes." But trust me when I tell you, if you deal directly with the cell phone jerks in the other areas of your life, like on the train or in a restaurant, you will be more able to *not* engage in a potential road rage incident. And, please, keep your hands on the wheel. I know it's so tempting to flip the proverbial bird when a jerk cuts you off, but most of the time, they don't see you anyway, so why be rude yourself?

2. If you can't beat 'em, make fun of 'em. Way back in 1998, when most cell phone users didn't know how to use their speed dial, Tom and Ray Magliozzi, the outspoken and hilarious Bostonians who host the popular NPR show "Car Talk," blazed the trail for the Rest of Us with the campaign "Drive Now, Talk Later." They call cell phone use while driving "immoral, unethical, inconsiderate, and downright stupid."

When the jerks have cut you off, go to the "Car Talk" website: http://cartalk.cars.com. You can send an e-mail or join a bulletin board discussion and rant in good company. Their archives have some truly priceless stories about cell phone jerks who drive.

Another website that can cheer you up when the jerks who drive kiss bumpers with you is www.SatireWire.com. This site has some hilarious send ups of cell phone jerks. Here's a brief excerpt from their tongue-in-cheek article entitled, "Car Phone Safety: Scream 'Aahh!' Before Impact":

Under pressure to do something about car accidents involving cell phones, the industry-backed Cell Phone Safety Council today launched a public service campaign urging users to "scream like hell" before impact, thereby alerting callers on the other end that there is some kind of trouble.

"It's ironic, but people who can talk forever on a cell phone suddenly come up mute when they're about to get into a collision," said CPSC spokesman Donald Lufrette. "They just get hit, and the caller on the other end doesn't know what happened."

Therefore, the safety council suggests users scream "Aahhh!" or "Oh, God!" just before impact. A proper scream, Lufrette insisted, can save your life, as the person on the other end of the call can then phone authorities . . ."

For more information on this story go to: www.satirewire.com/news/0007/satire-cellsafety.shtml.

3. Believe in a benevolent universal force that dislikes the jerks as much as the Rest of Us do. I found this absolute gem of cell phone jerk getting his due in the archive on the "Car Talk" website (www.cartalk.com). It was posted in 1999 and all I can say is that's the first time I ever wished I had been in a minivan.

I was approaching an equipment rental business in my aging Dodge minivan when a man who was talking on his cell phone . . . pulled out of the rental store parking lot right in front of me. I slammed on the brakes and managed to get the Caravan stopped. Annoyed, I slammed my hand down on the horn and held it there for a good while as he continued his left turn across a busy street! When I blew my horn, he attempted to lift the middle finger of his left hand (the hand holding the cell phone while propped up in the open window of his Blazer) toward me, and in so doing lost control of the phone, which flew out his open window directly toward me.

Wait, it gets better! The phone flew a short distance, bounced, and came to rest just in front of me. As I rolled forward, I heard the phone crunch under the left front, then the left rear tire of the van (a feat I couldn't duplicate in a hundred tries!). As I continued, I glanced in my rearview mirror and saw the remains of his cell phone in a small pile of high-tech particles on the street. Moral of the story: There is justice in the universe for those who talk on the cell phone while driving.

4. Don't just rant at the cell phone jerks, have some good comebacks prepared.

I have many friends who argue with me about this issue. They say, "It's not against the law," and I say, "Yes, but that doesn't mean it's okay and safe." I ask them if they've ever seen a bike courier riding in traffic on a cell phone. "Yes," they say, "that's just crazy." (Every one agrees about that one!) But a lot of bike riders (and rollerbladers too) do this now. It's not illegal either, but it sure doesn't seem safe to any of us who don't do it.

Others I know claim they simply can't manage their busy lives without using their drive time to make calls. Sorry, but ordering takeout on the way home just isn't worth the risk of causing an accident. What good is your take out if you never get there to pick it up?

Know the latest research studies so you can quote information from them. (See box on the next page for comebacks.)

Cell Phone Comebacks

Cell Phone Jerk: Talking on my cell phone is no more dangerous than tuning my radio or drinking coffee.

Comeback: Hmmmm ... then why don't we have a movement banning other distractions, like radios and coffee, and some of the most distracting passengers alive—children? According to the very latest research from the University of Utah's Psychology Department, your cognitive ability is impaired when having a conversation. The researchers concluded that, "In sum ... the use of cell phones disrupts driving performance by diverting attention from the information processing immediately associated with the safe operation of a motor vehicle." And researchers at the University of Rhode Island found that drivers who talk on cell phones while driving have a reduced field of vision.

Cell Phone Jerk: But I'm a good driver when I'm on my cell phone—it's the other people who can't do it.

Comeback: Ah, you've fallen right into my favorite trap. As I discuss at length on page 134, it's always the other guy. No, you just think you are a good driver. Don't people who are intoxicated think they're fine when they get behind the wheel? Again, the University of Utah researchers compared cell phone drivers with drivers who were legally intoxicated. The researchers found that the cell phone drivers exhibited greater impairment than the intoxicated drivers did.

Cell Phone Jerk: But I wear a headset (and/or I have the new "driving mode" feature on my cell).

Comeback: Sorry and surprise. The same University of Utah study found that "similar patterns of interference were observed for handheld and hands-free cell phones. These findings suggest that policies that restrict handheld devices but permit hands-free cell phone devices are not well-grounded in science." In Sweden, the National Road Administration studied the issue and concluded that it's ".... the distraction of the phone conversation [and not the phone itself] that is the problem."

That means that even a "driving mode" setting found on some of the newer state-of-the-art cell phones which verbally announces your calls and allows you to respond verbally—thereby reducing the need to take your hands from the wheel and your eyes from the road—really doesn't make cell phone use in the car safer either.

For more information on this University of Utah study of cell phones and driving, go to:
www.psych.utah.edu/AppliedCognitionLab/CogTechChapter.pdf.

To stay up to date on what research is being conducted and the results go to:
www.drivenowchatlater.com/Research_and_Studies.html.

JERKS WHO DRIVE AND THE LAW

From the Department of
Your Tax Dollars Taking a Vacation

In the year 2001, legislation to restrict mobile-phone use by drivers was proposed in forty-three states. A common misperception—probably fueled by the desire to live—is that many states have banned cell phone use while driving or are considering such legislation. In fact, no state completely bans the use of the cell phone while driving. So far, only New York State, The District of Columbia, and New Jersey have banned handheld cell phone use in cars.

To date, the federal government has not acted on the distracted driving issue. But if you visit the capital this inaction will make sense. All of the legislators and their assistants and the assistant's assistants are on cell phones. Who has time to pass legislation with all that talking going on?

For information on your where you state stands on enacting legislation, go to www.ncsl.org.

From the Department of
It Seems like It Would Be a No-Brainer:

If there's one person who should never, ever talk on a cell phone it's your child's bus driver, right? Wrong. Only seven states—Arizona, Arkansas, Illinois, Massachusetts, New Jersey, Rhode Island, and Tennessee—prohibit school bus drivers from using cell phones while operating the school bus.

From the Department of No Brains at All

Legislators in Massachusetts generally allow cell phone use, provided the driver keeps *at least one hand* on the steering wheel at all times. And I'm sure both eyes are on the road, right?

From the Department of
Have-You-Ever-Driven-with-a-Sixteen-Year-Old?

If there's a whole group of people who should never talk on a cell phone while driving, it's anyone who doesn't even have a driver's license, right? Wrong. Only Maine and New Jersey forbid drivers under age twenty-one who have only a learners' or instructional permit from using any type of cell phone while driving.

From the Department of Am-I-the-Only-One-Who-Finds-This-Suggestion-Ironic?

Because many people still hold cell phones while driving in New York City, legislators are proposing a toll-free number that other motorists can use to call (we assume on their cell phones) and report cell phone fanatics in action. Callers would report the time, date, location, and license plate number of the car being driven by the talker.

From the Department of Just Say No to Ham Sandwiches

According to a *USA Today* article the wireless industry believes that all distracted driving—that would include things like eating a ham sandwich or yelling at your children—should be addressed through education, not legislation.

From the Department of Your Deepest Suspicions Confirmed

Market Trends of Seattle found that drivers who earn more than $75,000 a year are far more likely than others to use cell phones while driving.

From the Department of Please, Throw Us a Bone

At least because the jerks are in their cars, we can't hear what they're saying. (Well, it's something.)

The Rest of the Jerks

Frank and Ernest

WELCOME TO
KINDERGARTEN
PLEASE TURN OFF
YOUR CELL PHONE

SCHOOL

It seems everywhere you look, there's a jerk on a cell phone. Yes, they're in restaurants, cars, and theaters. But let's face it, the cell phone jerks are everywhere we go: doctors' offices, hairdressers, bathrooms, hockey games, and even places of worship. Cell phone jerks are equal opportunity. They come in all ages, races, nationalities, and occupations. They remind us that no place is beyond the reach of being reachable and all tasks can be performed while talking on a cell phone.

73

> The Kid with a Scooby Doo Lunchbox

(I hate to call a kid a jerk, so let's say this boy is a possible jerk in the making.)

I teach the fifth grade. One day during class, I'm having a conversation with one of my students about a field trip. I told him we'd have to ask his parents. I turn my back and the next thing I hear is, "Mom, it's me Kyle. Can I go to the aquarium with my class?"

> The Jerk in the John

Leaving New York for California, I decide to make a stop at one of those rest areas on the side of the road. I go in the washroom. The first stall was taken so I went in the second stall. I just sat down when I hear a voice from the next stall say, "Hi there, how is it going?"

Okay, I am not the type to strike conversations with strangers in washrooms on the side of the road. I didn't know what to say so, finally, I say, "Actually, not bad."

Then the voice says, "So, what are you doing?"

I am starting to find that a bit weird, but I say, "Well, I'm going to California."

Then I hear the person say all flustered, "Look,

I'll call you back. Every time I ask you a question this idiot in the next stall keeps answering me."

Okay, this is a joke, but I have heard so many stories like this that it's clearly not far from the truth. If you hear a voice coming from the stall next door, you would think it's someone talking to you. People who talk while in the john are not only being rude to the person in the stall next door, they're exposing the person on the other end of the cell phone to bathroom noises—yuck.

➤ The Jerk with his Hand in the John

The Associated Press reported that a man riding a Metro-North train dropped his cell phone in a toilet and got his arm stuck trying to retrieve it. While police and firefighters were rescuing the man, thousands of commuters were delayed because the train sat blocking the platform.

➤ The Jerk in the Pew

A friend of mine was attending a church service. The hymn "You Are Holy: I Come in Silence" was being sung. The opening line for this hymn is the title and yes, you guessed it, right at that moment a cell phone rang.

Putting up a sign that another house of worship has used may help this church, *"Please turn off your cell phones, so God can hear your prayers."*

And speaking of being heard in church . . .

There was a man who was on cell phone during a service. During the final hymn, just as the music stopped, he said, "I gotta get the hell out of here. I can't hear a thing."

> The Jerk at the Pulpit

The *Shreveport Times* in Louisiana reported on a minister who, during his Sunday morning sermon, answered his own cell phone.

> The Jerk with the Dog

A guy in my neighborhood attaches his dog's leash to the back of his SUV. Then he drives slowly down the street while he talks on his cell phone. The dog must be used to it because he barks when he wants the guy to stop. I just hope he doesn't ever forget the dog is back there. That would not be a pretty site.

> The Jerk at the Funeral

A survey by SBC Communications found that 98

percent of cell phone users found it most inappropriate to use a wireless phone at a funeral. Here's a
story about one of the other 2 percent:

*At my mother's funeral, I was shocked to hear a cell
phone ring. I was even more floored when my
cousin answered it. She had a conversation during the service. She spoke so loudly the minister
had to shout over her voice.*

> The Jerk in the Santa Suit

During an interview, comedienne Janeane
Garofolo told Conan O'Brien, "I was walking on
Broadway, and there was a Santa, a Salvation
Army Santa, arguing with his girlfriend on a cell
phone. . . . It kinda weirded me out."

> The Jerk Giving a Speech

While hosting a fundraiser in 2002, hit movie
Rush Hour director Brett Ratner surprised many
guests by interrupting his own speech to take a
call on his cell phone. And, no, he wasn't trying to
be funny.

> The Jerk Ordering a Bagel

I was standing in line at my bagel place and I overheard a doctor phoning in a prescription for Viagra and he said the guy's name, he even spelled it. What if I had known the poor guy?

> The Jerk at the Dentist

A friend who is a dental hygienist told me this one:

I'm working on a patient in the chair and her cell phone rang. I told her that we asked our patients not to answer their phones. She said, "Oh, I can talk while you clean my teeth." So, she answered and proceeded to have a garbled conversation that the other person could not possibly have understood. I didn't know what else to say so I continued working as best I could. She even talked while I flossed her teeth.

> The Jerk Who Was the Dentist

My dentist capped my tooth while talking on his cell phone planning a golf outing—for the entire forty-five minutes. I don't think he said two words to me. He's affordable, so I still go back.

> The Jerk Who Told It to the Wrong Judge

A woman in Charleston, South Carolina made headlines for being thrown in jail for contempt of court. She failed to turn off her cell phone (after instructed to do so) and it rang during a sentencing hearing.

> The Jerk in the Elevator with the Sluggish Ovary

I thought the elevator was the last place of guaranteed silence in public. Who talks in elevators? But, no. A woman was in the elevator crying into her cell phone about her fertility problems. Like I really want to hear that one of her ovaries may not be working correctly and maybe she and her husband should forget the whole thing and adopt.

> The Jerk at the Mall

I was leaving the mall. There was a woman walking behind me who starts screaming, "You bastard . . . how could you?" I thought she was yelling at me for not holding the door for her or something. I turned around. She had a lot of hair, so I didn't see her headset. Naturally, I yelled back, "Hey, lady, calm down." Then she's yelling at me, "What are

you talking about?" At this point I realized she was
on the phone.

> The Jerk at Old Faithful

There I was on my vacation in Yellowstone
National Park. I'm hiking up a trail and I heard
yelling. I was startled, thinking someone needed
help. Then I get closer and I see a guy on the phone
apparently yelling at his stockbroker. I don't get it.
You come here to get away. If you need to discuss
business, stay home, or at least talk quietly.

> The Jerk in the Cartoon

You know cell phones are part of the culture when
even my son's favorite cartoon character, Bob the
Builder, has a cell phone and it's often important
to the plot, like when Spud the Scarecrow (don't
ask) took it and sent Bob and the gang into a
searching frenzy.

> The Jerk at the Four Seasons

A friend was trying to check into a very nice
hotel in New York. The man in front of her in line
was having two conversations. One with the front

desk clerk and the other with the person on his cell phone.

The front desk clerk at times had to wait until he had finished his sentence with the person on the cell phone before he could respond to her. He was really holding up the line. Another person in line said, "If you hung up, we'd all get checked in faster." The man on the phone turned and said to him, "It's an important call."

The man was now having three conversations.

As I mentioned earlier, the bad news is that I didn't have a lot of difficulty collecting these stories. The good news is that from a global perspective we are not alone. The following stories come from around the world.

➤ The Jerk with a Shotgun

It seems hunters in Finland—the home of Nokia phones—are strapping cell phones in pouches to the backs of their hunting hounds. Then, with simple tracking devices beamed toward satellites that are part of the GPS system, the hunters can tell within yards where the dog is running by looking at a hand held GPS screen . . . the dog could be ten, twenty, one hundred miles away. The hunter still knows precisely whether the dog is chasing bear or elk, lapping up water from a creek or stopped to relieve himself.

Additionally, the hunter is able to transmit, through a cell phone of his own, instructions to the dog.

"How long's this pit stop going to take, Blue?"

SOURCE: Garvey Winegar,
Richmond Times Dispatch, September 2002

➤ The Jerk in the Coffin

The European news service Annaova reported that mourners at a chapel in Belgium were shocked when a mobile phone started ringing inside the coffin. Some members of the family were so startled they ran outside while the undertaker had to reopen the coffin to empty the dead man's pockets.

➤ The Jerk in the Tree

A seventy-eight-year-old Romanian woman climbs a tree twice a week to use her mobile phone. The woman says that climbing the twenty-foot tree is the only way to get a signal in her village. She climbs the tree and waits for her grandchildren to call her. Yet, sometimes she climbs for nothing. "Two weeks ago, my grandson . . . was supposed to call . . . I waited in the tree for an hour," the grandmother said, "but no one called."

(In this case, the grandson is a jerk, too.)

SOURCE: Nick Farrell, www.vnunet.com, July 8, 2002

> The Jerk Who Leaned Over at the Zoo

UPI reported that a man in England was shocked to see a three-foot catfish eat his $500 cell phone after he dropped it in a zoo fish tank.

"There were about fifty people around the pool asking me to ring it to see which fish vibrated," he said. Marwell Zoo curator Peter Bircher said he had a look inside the fish's mouth but was unable to retrieve it. "The next morning the phone was found at the bottom of the pool," he said. "The fish is well and the phone was returned."

(Yes, but would you really want it back?)

> The Even Bigger Jerk at the Zoo

In March of 2000, Reuters reported that a twenty-five-year-old Mexican man miraculously escaped with only minor injuries after a lion attacked him as he tried to retrieve a cell phone in the creature's cage. Guillermo Orozco received injuries to his chest, back, and face when he entered the cage of "Zeus" at an amusement park in Pachuca in the central Mexican state of Hidalgo.

Reforma, Mexico's daily newspaper, reported that the Pachuca resident had been drinking (what a surprise) and made a wager with a friend that he could recover his phone before climbing into the cage.

> The Jerk Who Was the Judge

A judge in Delhi's high court was forced to confiscate his own cell phone after it rang during a hearing. The red-faced judge handed over his phone and threatened to report himself to the High Court Bar Committee—the course of action he would have taken if a lawyer's phone had gone off. Fair's fair.

> The Jerk in the Movie

In China, one of the hottest movies this year was *Cell Phone*, in which a woman catches her lover cheating when she intercepts a message on his cell phone. In the movie, an unfaithful jerk deceives his wife and his girlfriends through cellular means.

Even the fields and courts of the world of sports are not safe from the jerks, as the following stories prove:

> The Jerk with the Lamb

Iulica Traznea, the Romanian soccer player, was about to cross the ball in a match against Victoria Valea Ramnicului when his cell phone rang.

To the amazement of the referee and other players, he then spent five minutes trying to sell one of the lambs from his farm to a prospective buyer.

Eventually, the referee sent him off the field and the club is preparing disciplinary action against him.

Traznea said, "If they paid us enough in the first place we would not have to get involved in other things."

> The Jerk at Wimbledon

On July 3, 2000, Monica Seles stopped playing midway through a Wimbledon match to complain about a distracting noise coming from the audience. You guessed it—ringing cell phones were interfering with her ability to concentrate.

(In spite of the jerks, she went on to win.)

> The Jerk with Unfortunate Good Aim

Fan rage via cell phone is on the rise. And no, I don't mean reaching out and calling someone to tell them off. I mean reaching out and hurling your phone into the head of a player you're steamed at.

This happened to Rangers outfielder Carl Everett, who was clocked in the head by a disgruntled cell phone fan.

> The Jerk Who Made a Touchdown

Joe Horn, the New Orleans wide receiver, caused quite a scandal by celebrating a touchdown by pulling a hidden cell phone from the padding protecting the goal post. He said he was calling his mother and children. He was later fined $30,000 for the incident.

Still, there are indications Horn's cell phone antics could pay off for him. Cell phone companies have reportedly approached him regarding possible commercial tie-ins.

Could You Be a Jerk, Jerk, too?

Tell the truth:

1. Has someone responded to your cell phone conversation as if you were talking to him or her?

2. Have you stopped a face-to-face conversation with a friend to have a cell phone conversation?

3. Have you ever carried on two conversations at once, with the caller on the cell phone and the person you were doing business with (cashier, order taker, etc.)?

4. Is your cell phone always on when you're out?

5. Do you automatically tell people, "Call me anytime?" (Do you really want them to call you at 3 AM?) Or "You can always reach me on my cell." (Always? Don't you sleep? Don't you take a shower? Don't you chew food? Don't you have a life away from your cell phone?) If you answered yes to any of these questions, you might be a cell phone jerk too. Read on.

The Seven Habits of Highly Annoying Multi-taskers

1. Have no respect for other people's time and be sure to rub their faces in it.

A cell phone jerk was asked by her hairdresser to turn off her cell phone because the hairdresser couldn't cut her hair—she was talking so much, she interfered with her hairdresser's ability to cut. She was also causing the hairdresser's other clients to wait even longer.

Guess what? The cell phone jerk accused the hairdresser of being rude. Bet you didn't see that coming.

2. Ignore all the "little people" you can, especially cashiers and receptionists.

I was behind a woman in the check-out line at the grocery store who was talking on her cell phone. She was so busy talking and trying to hold her phone that she was very slow in putting her groceries on the belt. Then the cashier said, "Paper or plastic?" No answer. But she held up her finger to indicate, "Hold on, I'll be right with you."

"Paper or plastic?" the cashier asked again. Finally, the man behind me said, "Put the paper over her head and the groceries in plastic." Everyone laughed. The woman never hung up.

3. Overcome obstacles, even water.

... there I was at the downtown YMCA stepping in for a post-swim shower when it became apparent that the only other shower-room inhabitant, a guy diagonally across from me, was talking non-stop. Actually, bellowing was more like it ...

That's right, you guessed it. He was yakking away on a cell phone. With a towel over his head. In the shower. Did I say the man was yakking away on a cell phone with a towel over his head in the shower? What I meant to say is, he was multi-tasking. And you thought he was just being a roaring, screaming jerk.

Source: Peter Leo, Pittsburgh Post Gazette

4. Make mobile multi-tasking a family affair, that way your kids won't notice that you're ignoring them.

As a treat, we took our two teenage sons out to a nice restaurant. We were stunned to see a family of five sitting near us who were all on cell phones having separate conversations. Even the little girl who couldn't have been more than twelve-years old was talking on a little pink flip phone that glittered and flashed when it rang, which it did about four times. The waitress was going crazy trying to get their order. Afterward, in the car, my fourteen-year-old son said, "It's not fair. You always make us talk to each other."

5. Have conversations just for the heck of it.

"Hi, it's me. I'm on the train. Can you hear me? What are you doing? Yes, I can hear you. What's for dinner? Can you still hear me? What? What did you say? What's peek cloth? What? I can't hear you? That's better. Oh, meat loaf. Sounds good. I said, sounds . . . Wait, we're going into a tunnel so if we get disconnected I'll call you back. Did you hear me? I'll call you back. Are you there?"

"Hi, it's me again. Can you hear me now? We got disconnected. I said, meat loaf sounds good. I said, "Meat loaf sounds good." See you in about half an hour. A half an hour. Right. Half an hour. Love you, too. Bye."

6. Accept, or simply refuse to notice, that others disdain you.

A friend, who is a reporter, sent me this story in an e-mail:

So, I'm walking up Fifteenth Street yesterday morning, going to work, and in front of me is a guy who is trying to juggle four different things—bottle of juice, bag of something, briefcase, and, of course, his cell phone, because he has to try to conduct a conversation while herking-jerking his whole little circus up the street.

The cell phone slips out of his hand—bam! Hits the sidewalk and breaks into about six pieces.

I'll tell ya, just seeing that, it made me so happy. I practically giggled. I can't remember the last time some random city occurrence so pleased me. He's down on the sidewalk, trying to piece his broken cell phone together.

The best part was, when I reached Race Street, I noticed he's now on the other side of the street, holding this little wreck of plastic and wires together, trying to make it work: "Hello? Hello? Hello?"

As Homer Simpson would say, "Schweeeeeeeeet."

7. Learn how to drive with your elbows or knees in the biggest car you can find.

"In another incident, a [bus] driver was seen with a hand on his phone on a rainy day, and what appeared to be only elbows on the steering wheel ..."

SOURCE: NBC6, South Florida News

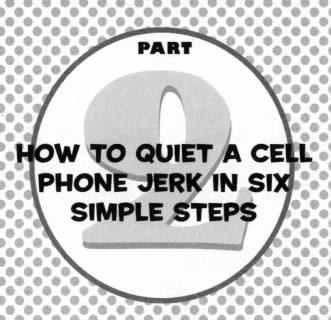

HOW TO QUIET A CELL PHONE JERK IN SIX SIMPLE STEPS

Once a new technology rolls over you, if you're not part of the steamroller, you're part of the road.

**—STEWART BRAND
ENVIRONMENTALIST, FUTURIST
FOUNDER OF THE *WHOLE EARTH
CATALOG***

Speed Bump

www.cartoonistgroup.com

Stop Complaining and Do Something

My wife and I were at dinner. There was a man on a cell phone at a nearby table. He was very loud. We were so annoyed. So were the people at the table next to us. We ended up talking to them about how sick we were of the cell phone jerks. Then our waiter came over and he started telling us his horror stories. We all agreed that they are ruining our dining experience. Why doesn't someone do something?

When I asked the man who told me the story on page 95, "Why didn't you say something?" he said, "We did, to the people at the next table and our waiter."

"No," I said, "I mean, why didn't you say something to the cell phone jerk?"

"Well, um . . . you see . . . actually, Barbara . . . what would I have . . . but what if? . . . I guess I don't know."

The very first thing to understand when you cross paths with a cell phone jerk is to realize that you *can* speak up and say something.

Yet, for many people who have never had assertiveness training—and that's a lot of us—being assertive and saying something to the jerk is often really, surprisingly, even shockingly, hard. As I discuss in my book, *The Power of Positive Confrontation*, it really can be okay to express yourself to others, including the cell phone jerks around you, as long as you are, yes, you guessed it, polite and powerful about it.

Yet, many of us go through life thinking that when it comes to the jerky behavior of others that we have to accept it because:

> That's just the way it is—people are rude and life isn't fair.
> We don't know what to say.
> We're afraid of the reaction we might get from the jerk if we do say something. (Which can be a legitimate concern, at times, especially if the jerk is cracking his hairy knuckles or walking her hungry-looking Doberman Pincher.)

Then there are others who do take action against the cell phone jerks, but blow it because they:

> Beat around the bush and then apologize, saying something like, "Gee, sorry to bother you, I really am, but could you lower your voice? I have a horrible headache, the doctors don't know why . . ." (In other words, you wimp out.)
> Lose their tempers and become jerks themselves, by yelling things like, "Shut up, for the love of all that is holy and sacred in the universe, just shut up!" (You're very aggressive, not to mention rather dramatic.)
> Really lose it and end up in jail. (Like the supreme jerks in the box on page 100.)

You may be thinking, *"Hold on a minute. I don't actually want to say anything to the jerks, I just want to complain about them."*

As I say in my seminars, I would encourage you to rethink that position. Here are the reasons why we need to stop complaining and, when the situation is right, speak up to the cell phone jerks and PEG'em:

1. Complaining can be fun, but nobody changes. When complaining about cell phone jerks you can bond with people you would never normally bond with, like your waiter or the other annoyed people on your train. Yes, complaining can make the time go faster when you're getting your hair cut or waiting in line at the bank, but let's face it, complaining is not going to get us any real, lasting relief from the jerks, especially when the people we complain to are people who already agree with us.

2. Being annoyed all the time stresses you out and diminishes the quality of your life. It's not fun to feel like you can't ride to work in peace, or go out to dinner or a movie, without being subjected to loud ringtones belting out songs you don't want to hear and ruining the ones you do want to hear. Don't you hate it when you get home and you think, "I wish I'd said something," or "If only I knew what to say . . ." and then you feel badly about yourself because you didn't?

3. How long can you bite your tongue before you do permanent taste bud damage? There is an eventual consequence for a lot of people who hold their tongues for too long. You stew. You steam. You can't take it anymore and then one day you explode. The next thing you know, you're reprising Linda Blair's role in the movie *The Exorcist*—you're turning green and spewing diabolical expletives out of your mouth. It happens. Though going "kaboom" may feel powerful when you're exploding and spewing, it's not. It's just rude and aggressive. Plus, you have given the jerk power over you. He or she has caused you to lose it. Ironically, you're now a jerk, too.

4. Taking action can help you achieve cell phone jerk serenity. In other words, you can learn to pick your conflicts. When you deal with and PEG the jerks you can, the jerks you can't deal with, or don't choose to deal with, don't bother you as much.

To all of you who are waiting for someone else to take care of the cell phone jerk problem: The jerks aren't going to change until we help them change. But don't panic, there are many ways to do this without having to take a week long seminar, self-defense classes, or join a ten-step program, though there are steps for you to follow—six in all. These steps will help you to become more polite and powerful when you encounter a cell phone jerk. Read on . . .

Backlash Gone Bad

Unfortunately, there seems to be a disturbing trend towards cell phone bashing. It's the "Kaboom Effect" except on a more extreme and violent level. I know you would never do anything like the stories I'm about to share, but it's undeniable, and a little frightening, that cell phone rage is growing. There's even a website that has been widely publicized dedicated to cell phone stomping. Two men wearing giant cell phone suits (which they admit to having stolen from a video shoot) sneak up on cell phone users, grab their cell phones, and smash them to bits. Here are my picks for the "worst of the worst" cell phone revenge horror stories ever:

✱ The Crazed Cab Driver:

Victoria's Secret model Laetitia Casta made headlines around the world, not for her million-dollar face, but for being doused with tear gas by an irate Parisian cab driver. The cabbie later told police that he was sick of listening to the incessant ringing of the model's cell phone.

As my Uncle Seymour would say, "Was he insane or what?" Yes, this cab driver was probably insane and, thankfully, Ms. Casta recovered.

✱ Movie Mayhem:

A cell phone jerk in Dorchester, Massachusetts, was asked to put his cell phone away by another viewer during a horror movie. (How appropriate for what's to come.) He wouldn't. The viewer then put his feet on the back of the jerk's seat (thereby becoming a jerk himself). The cell phone jerk then pulled out a knife and stabbed the man in the foot with a knife. Luckily the man's shoe took the brunt of the stabbing.

✳ More Movie Mayhem:

This very rude girl—a teenager, I think—was talking on her cell phone during the movie. She ignored the shushes from the people all around her. Finally, a man got up, stomped down the aisle, and dumped a soda on her. We knew this was what happened because we could hear the splash and then she ran up the aisle dripping wet and crying. A lot of people clapped. The police ended up being called. I don't know if they arrested the guy who threw the cup but I know they came and got him out of his seat.

✳ Hell Hath No Fury:

In December 2003, the Associated Press reported that an apparently irate Filipino housewife sliced off her husband's penis while he slept. The reason? She discovered text messages from another woman on his mobile phone.

A local radio station reported that the woman rushed her husband to hospital in Manila but that she forgot to bring the severed piece of flesh. (Oops.)

"Doctors were doubtful they would be able to reattach his severed flesh after she raced home to collect the missing pice. The man, a plumber, told the radio station he had forgiven his wife."

Callers to the station, reacting to the news, offered

helpful hints to wayward husbands, such as never sleeping on their backs and always keeping mobile phones tucked under the pillow.

Source: Whiteboard News, December 11, 2003

✳ Fast Food Fracas:

When I read this story on *The Restaurant Report,* an industry website, I thought maybe we're safer when ordering our food "to go":

> *A guest was speaking loudly on his cell phone during lunch in one of our fast-food restaurants. He was asked by another couple to lower his voice, he ignored them and they left. Two other men walked over to this cell user's table. They shouted at the talker and tried to grab his cell phone. In the scuffle the cell user and his companion were punched in the nose and face. The attackers then fled the scene. The two men refused medical treatment and did not press charges, but the incident was described in the local paper. The cell user said, "I won't be using my cell phone in restaurants anymore."*
> *Source: www.restaurantreport.com*

Understand Why the Jerks Are Jerks

I was in a romantic restaurant about to propose to my girlfriend, when this jerk at the next table starts having a loud cell phone conversation. What is he thinking? Doesn't he see the roses? Doesn't he see the champagne bucket? Doesn't he get it? What is this guy thinking? That's what I really wanted to know.

Though you may think you don't care or it doesn't matter, if we're going to deal with the jerks, the first thing we need to understand is why they're jerks in the first place. Understanding the behavior of cell phone jerks will help you to choose whether or not to take action against one and how you'll handle yourself when you do.

The five reasons that follow, do not, repeat do not excuse their rude behavior, it's just that as my husband the lawyer might say, "There are mitigating circumstances . . ."

THE JERKS YELL DUE TO AN EVOLUTIONARY FLAW

A woman on my train was talking very loudly, explaining to her child how to make macaroni and cheese for dinner. An annoyed passenger leaned over and told her, "Can you please lower your voice? You're very loud." She responded, "But I can't hear her!"

The above joke is not really a joke. Unfortunately, it's a great example of human nature and technology colliding in a negative way and the result is: Cell Yell.

Cell Yell is the vocal tendency among the majority of cell phone jerks to talk too loudly, yell, shout, and even scream. "Why?" the Rest of Us ask. "Why? Why? Why do they do it?"

If every one knows that the number one complaint about cell phone users is that they talk too loudly, why don't people quiet down?

Here is why: Illogically, people believe that if they can't hear, then the other person must not be able to hear also. So they raise their voices and become jerks. People who are hard of hearing often do this when speaking to people who are not hard of hearing. It just happens. Really, it does. I believe it's human nature, some evolutionary flaw that must have served a purpose when we lived in caves. (Maybe grunting loudly for no apparent reason was viewed as a prehistoric leadership skill.) We mistakenly let our volume compensate for a lack of hearing.

I used to teach English as a second language. It is amazing the number of Americans who will shout at non-English speaking people because they automatically and illogically think that their lack of ability to understand English words is a hearing issue.

Three Additional Reasons Why People Shout into Cell Phones:

1. Phone booths weren't just for Superman. Little glass rooms were built around phones to block out background noise that affects your ability to hear the person you were speaking with.

2. It's a cell phone, not a landline. Though they may be out there, I have yet to experience a cell phone that is as good as a landline. People will tell me, "Mine is great. You can't tell the difference," and yet they often sound like they're talking to me while eating a donut with a bag on their head. Though the technology will probably get there, it's not, judging from the success of Verizon's "Can you hear me now" commercial, there yet.

3. Forget the money, show me the volume control. The jerks don't know how to raise the volume on their phones so they can hear the other person better. (Why? They never take the time to read their manual.) But now that the newest cell phones come with the volume buttons right on the side of the phone, the jerks are running out of excuses on this one.

A Philosophical Discussion on Why People Shout into Cell Phones

René Descartes

I have a cell phone, therefore I am. If I shout into my cell phone, therefore I am even more.

Emily Dickinson

A train went through a burial gate
A bird broke forth and sang
And trilled, and quivered, and shook his throat
Till a cell phone rang and a cell phone jerk sang
And trilled quite loudly.

Jean-Paul Sartre

Man will never speak softly into a cell phone unless he has first understood that he must count on no one to hear him. He is alone, abandoned on earth, without help, only to one day die. How depressing . . . arrrrghhhh!

Andy Rooney

Did you ever notice how some people shout in their cell phones? I think the wireless industry has a lot of explaining to do.

Wireless Industry Spokeswoman

People aren't shouting. They're excited. Technology is exciting. Of course we support consumer education but the fact is that perception is a large part of the problem.

George W. Bush

It will be a long battle to get people to lower their voices on cell phones. It will be a costly battle. But make no mistake; the American people are a determined people. In the war against the loud speakers on cell phones the American people will prevail.

Donald Rumsfeld

What we know is that the cell phone jerks don't know that we know they're loud because they don't know their manuals.

The Dalai Lama

When the loud speaker is ready to speak properly into a cell phone, his volume button will appear.

Sigmund Freud

Every shout in a cell phone represents not a desire to have sex with one's mother, but rather a desire to return to the womb where one can scream without fear of reprisal from the father.

THE JERKS DON'T KNOW
HOW TO USE THEIR PHONES

*I have to keep my phone on, because I don't know how
to put it on vibrate.*

—A surgeon who wishes to remain anonymous
(perhaps because he can take out an appendix,
but he can't work his phone)

Be honest, tell me you've read the thirty-page miniature
manual that came with your cell phone?

Didn't you make a mistake or two when you first used
your cell phone in public? Remember the learning curve
you experienced? Many people are rude on cell phones
simply because they don't know how to operate them.

"Oops! Sorry, Ned. I guess I dialed you by mistake."

Younger people usually don't have this problem, yet many of us who weren't born in the 1990s do indeed have issues. I for one love technology but I still don't know how to program my VCR to tape a TV show unless it's in real time and on channel three. (And now I have to learn how to work a DVD.)

There are some super considerate people, maybe ten or eleven, out of the millions of cell phone users, who actually turn their phones off because they don't know how to silence them or put them on vibrate. Clearly these eleven people are not in the majority, are they?

No matter what your age or technological comfort level, not knowing how to work your cell phone is not an excuse for poor cell phone behavior. Read the manual or ask someone for help. If you're really challenged, buy a new cell phone with an "etiquette setting" right on the key pad.

Fantasy Cell Phone Island

Here are my fantasy solutions to people being rude because they don't know how to work their phones. Success depends upon the cooperation of the cell phone industry (and I do applaud many of them for getting involved in cell phone courtesy promotion) but it's time to take it to the next level.

Cell Phone Licensing Test: Cell sellers would not make a sale until the buyer has passed a simple test. This test would involve just two questions: 1) How do you put the phone on vibrate? and 2) How do you raise and lower the volume? (If the salesperson wanted to give a lecture on annoying ringtones and why they should be avoided, I, for one, wouldn't complain.)
This would be similar to getting a driver's license, only the picture on your cell phone license would be much more flattering.

Cell Phone Butlers: If Gyweneth Paltrow, Madonna, and other celebs can purchase a Vertu cell phone, Nokia's luxury line that sells for a mere $20,000 and comes with a concierge service, the equivalent of a cell phone butler, why can't the Rest of Us have a simpler, bargain version? (I, for one don't need sapphires embedded on my phone. Being old-fashioned, I prefer them on rings and necklaces.) Instead of getting us tickets to the opera or restaurant reservations, our butlers would simply act as live cell phone monitors—CPBs, for short (Whew, there are a lot of acronyms with technology.) to monitor our volume. If we were too loud in public, they would politely interrupt us to let us know, saying, "Please lower your voice."

Priority Call Message Button: Whenever my son calls me on his cell phone, I feel like I have to answer it because what if he's in trouble? Of course, it's usually, "I had a birdie on hole two." This is nice news but unless it's a hole in one, it can wait. With a priority call message button, (e-mail has a similar feature) the caller can let you know how urgent they think the call is. (Of course, you may not agree with the level of urgency, but it may help with some calls.)

A much more realistic possibility, though, is to use technology—the cause and solution to many of our cell phone jerk problems—to program phones for people. As I mentioned on page 40, there is technology—Q-Zone—in development that will automatically silence cell phone ringers in designated areas.

THE JERKS ARE INFATUATED

▌believe that what happens to a lot of people is that they get infatuated with their cell phone. I say, "infatuated" and not "in love" because love lasts and infatuation, as I'm sure you've experienced sometime in high school, wears off—eventually.

Let's face it, even if you hate cell phones (I don't) and don't own one (I do) you have to admit the technology is convenient and even remarkable. There's a lot to love.

These love-at-first-sight cell users are the people who are both inexperienced and smitten with their phones. And, as you probably know, in that starry-eyed condition, you really don't notice others around you and how you may be annoying them. It's just you and your cell phone out in the world . . . ahhhhh . . . isn't technology grand?

The good news is that many cell phone infatuations die out because being in constant touch wears these lovers out. Or, there's an even swifter wake-up call—the first cell phone bill. (There's even a television commercial of a screaming man being taken to the hospital because he opened his cell phone bill.) Yes, there's just nothing like shelling out $350 for the privilege of asking all your friends, "Where are you?" and telling them, "I'm in the bookstore," to turn love into a lukewarm friendship.

Here are what some reformed cell phone jerks told me

about the moment they realized the cell phone honeymoon was over:

From Indispensable to Enslavement

I admit it, I got carried away. I was always available and I liked that. My cell phone made me feel like I was more indispensable at work—if you're always available you are the "go-to guy." Then one weekend evening during dinner my boss called me and I had to answer it (or at least call him back right away) because he knew I always had it on. I was tired and really needed a break from work. It hit me then that my cell phone wasn't a godsend. It was a leash and my boss was holding it.

From Peace of Mind to Giving Him a Piece of Your Mind

I wanted my teenage son to have a cell phone, so he could be in touch with me and so I would always know where he was at all times. He said he understood it was for important calls and emergency calls only. I almost fainted when his first cell phone bill came in and it had over 815 minutes of airtime on it. That is over thirteen hours on the phone! Knowing exactly where he was at all times came in very handy—I was able to immediately confiscate his phone and ground him for the rest of his life.

From Free Phone to Free Me From My Phone

As a political consultant I was thrilled when my company bought and paid for a cell phone. I used it constantly, especially in the car during my hour-long commute. I thought it was the greatest invention since salad in a bag. It wasn't until I left that job and had to pay for my own cell phone and began using it a lot less that I realized how attached, like an umbilical cord, I had become. It was so nice to sit in my car and just listen to the radio again or just have some time to think. I feel very liberated.

So much for the good news. The bad news: Even though many cell phone jerks reform on their own, with so many new users signing up, the reformed jerks are being replaced by new people who are now infatuated or who don't know how to use their phones or both. This is an ongoing cycle but I do believe we'll reach the ultimate saturation point and then things will steadily and finally improve. Yes, I'm an optimist.

Some Jerks Learn the Hard Way ...
But They Do Learn

Some cell phone jerks overcome their infatuation without intervention from the Rest of Us. It's one thing to be a jerk, it's another to look like one.

When Cell Phones Dial Themselves

Okay, I was one of those people who always had to have my phone on, just in case. Once, I was out on a date I accidentally pushed my mom's speed dialed button and didn't know it. The next day she called me and said, "So how was your hamburger last night?" I was like, "How do you know what I ate last night?" She loved telling me what had happened. I felt like my mom had been out on a date with me. I didn't want to know what else she heard. I now turn my cell phone off when I am with a girl.

Phones dialing themselves inside your pocket or pocketbook is the kind of story you hear more and more. A woman I met told me that she divorced her husband because he accidentally called her while he was with his mistress and didn't know the phone was on. I heard of another woman whose husband hadn't realized he was still connected to his wife while he made plans to go to an adult club with his friend who was in the car. So when your cell phone is on, be careful what you say.

When Cell Phones Don't Want to Get Pregnant

Yes, I was one of those people who always whipped their cell phone out in a meeting so I could call and get information right away or to take calls. Then during one very tense meeting, I whipped it out of my purse to call my assistant for some budget numbers and to my horror, I discovered that I was holding my birth control pills up to my ear.

Additional moral of the story: Leave your birth control at home.

When Cell Phones Are the Least of Someone's Problem

My boss told me I was going to get fired if I didn't stop talking on my cell phone at work. How humiliating. A year ago, I was told to stop surfing the web. Six months ago, I was told to stop using e-mail for personal correspondence. I wonder what's next?

Starting your own business perhaps?

When Cell Phones Help You Lose an Election

In November 2000, the Republican businessman Jack E. Robinson challenged the Democratic incumbent (Ted Kennedy) for a seat in the U.S. Senate. His campaign started with a bang, literally—while doing a live interview via a cell phone in his car, listeners suddenly heard a crash. Robinson had gotten into an accident.

Though no one was seriously injured and Mr. Robinson didn't cause the accident, it sure looked bad.

When You Need Your Cell Phone to Call a Lawyer

My wife told me she would divorce me if I didn't stop using my cell phone all the time. I don't think she would have, but she did hide it a few times but when she ran it through the dishwasher, I got it. It was a problem.

When Steaks Attack

A waiter told me this story:

One of my regular customers is a nice guy, but he always talks on his cell phone while he's sitting there. One day, I'm walking by his table. He's got the phone wedged into his shoulder and he's trying to keep it there and cut his steak. It didn't work out too well. The steak came flying off his plate and landed on my shoe. Ever since that happened, he now turns his phone off and actually eats during dinner.

THE JERKS ARE ADDICTED

Once you get the handsets that send messages, you can create an addiction because you have this instant, always-on, nationwide, wherever-you-go ability to receive and send a message.

—Richard Vile, Director of Messaging, Verizon Wireless

Some jerks don't recover from their infatuation. In fact, their fondness and attachment grows and grows until finally the jerk is hooked. I'm certainly no expert on addiction but it's obvious people are addicted to their cell phones, when:

1. There's a support group for it.

It was only a matter of time, but the first cell phone anonymous support group has been formed. A Decatur psychotherapist, Hugh Burns said on the Citizen website (www.citizenonline .net) that he made the decision to start one after he witnessed five people talk on cell phones during a church service. (I wonder if those five churchgoers will show up for the first meeting.)

Unfortunately, there's no official diagnosis for cell phone dependency so any treatment would have to paid out-of-pocket, but considering some cell phone bills I've heard about it, it might be a savings.

2. People would rather give up their wallets if mugged.

A 2002 survey by the mobile information company WapOneline reported that 86 percent of the respondents say that they feel anxious when they are without their cell phones. So anxious that if mugged, 75 percent would rather hand over their wallets than lose their cell phones.

Personally, I just can't imagine telling a mugger, "Anything, just not my cell. Look I have an ATM card and I just made a hefty deposit this morning. Do you have a pen? Let me write down my PIN number for you. And here are my car keys. Yes, it's parked right over there. I just had it washed this morning. If you could do me a favor and baby the clutch a little when you start it, that would be great."

3. Dr. Phil is doing shows about it.

On his show, Dr. Phil has said that cell phoneaholics send two messages to others: "People that do this are amazingly insecure, needing to be constantly validated," and "They're hiding behind these calls, saying, 'I can be with you but talk to somebody else, that way I can't get real and intimate with you because I'm here but I'm not.'"

Ouch.

One couple, Todd and Kelly were having serious relationship problems because of Todd's cell phone addiction. Kelly described it by saying: "I do feel like he's cheating with the cell phone." Todd's cell phone even rang while Dr. Phil was interviewing him.

Dr. Phil got Todd to commit to giving up his cell phone for thirty days. This is how Kelly described the complete change in their marriage *sans* cell phone:

Our life has just turned completely around and it's wonderful. We've become like we were before we got married: best friends. He treats me like a queen. Thank you, Dr. Phil, for getting my husband's cell phone unglued from his ear.

Now, if Todd would just stop leaving his socks on the floor, this couple could really take a second honeymoon.

SOURCE: www.drphil.com

4. There's a new name for it.

A recent article by Miki Tanikawa in the *International Herald Tribune*, entitled "Addicted on a Cellular Level," says that young cell phone users have fallen into *Keichu*, a type of cell phone addiction, which is "acquiring an unstoppable habit of e-mailing or 'texting' friends, playing games, and downloading pictures and music."

Chikara Kato, professor of linguistics and communications at Japan's Sugiyama Jogakuin University, said such addicts typically become restless and irritated when deprived of their handsets. There are reports that some young workers, who are unable to quit phone e-mailing while at work, have lost their jobs, he said, adding, "This is serious."

I agree with Professor Kato; if you're getting fired, that's a problem.

5. People compare cell phones with cigarettes.

I'm sure it twists the battery charger cords of cell phone jerks when people compare cell phone addiction with cigarette addiction. But there's even research to support the notion.

A report published in the *British Medical Journal* (November 2000) claimed that cigarettes are slowly being replaced by an equally addictive obsession—the cell phone. Most notably that a rise in mobile phone use during the late 1990s coincided with a decline in smoking among fifteen-year-olds. The researchers noted that cell phones have many of the same traits that attract teens to cigarettes: a sense of individuality and sociability, a desire to rebel, and the need to bond with friends.

And . . . the researchers pointed out that "the marketing of the mobile phone is rooted in promoting self-image and identity, which resembles cigarette advertising."

The upside for the cell phone jerks is that at least cell phones don't damage your health unless you're driving and have an accident. The bad news for the Rest of Us: Our health suffers due to stress-induced second-hand chat.

Might As Well Face It, We're Addicted to Phone

Addiction comes in all forms. Here's how a college student described the agony of losing her cell phone:

> If I told you that I was a bit frazzled, it would be the under-statement of the century ... I quickly became panic-stricken, worried that my friends and family wouldn't be able to get in touch with me in case of an emergency. Thoughts of accidents, heart attacks, terrorism, natural disasters, and general death and destruction raced through my head ...
>
> SOURCE: University Wire, January 27, 2004

And another college student:

> I also have a cell phone addiction, and I think it's high time we all fessed up to it and got on the road to recovery.
>
> Step one is admitting you have a problem. Gigantic monthly bills, using the term "roll-over" when not addressing a dog and, finally, calluses on your ear are classic symptoms ...
>
> SOURCE: University Wire, October 3, 2003

Here, an exasperated mom in my son's school details his addiction:

> How do I know cell phone use is an addiction? My son walks our dog around the block. He takes his cell phone with him and calls me to ask what's for dinner.

But, what if students were made to say "no" to cell phones? As this story shows, many chose to just say no!:

A Rutgers University professor, Sergio Chaparro, who teaches "Introduction to Information Technology and Informatics" at the university's News Brunswick, New Jersey campus, asked his students to stop using their cell phones for forty-eight hours.

The results: only three students made it through the forty-eight hours but they did admit they were anxious to turn them back on and get their messages. (The class was also asked if they would shut off their phones for $50. The majority answered yes. So maybe that's another way to get people to turn off their cell phones—pay them.)

SOURCE: *University Newswire, April 5, 2000.*

Cell phone addiction is not just for the young:

A Toronto man, who once considered himself above high-tech toys said this of his new camera cell phone:

It's kind of embarrassing, but I can't stop using it. It's really, really fun. . . . Now my wife is hooked, too, and two of my friends have gone out to buy their own. It's crazy how the technology is advancing, and how addictive it can be.

SOURCE: *The Gazette*, Montreal, Quebec

The Ten Signs That
You're Addicted to Your ce...

1. You say, "I can leave it home anytime I want'
   never do.

2. You spend $200 to have crystal and stone de...
   tions applied to your cell phone when your electric
   bill is overdue.

3. Your response to a scientific study proving once and
   for all that cell phones cause brain cancer would be,
   "We've all gotta go sometime."

4. You call your husband to say, "Honey, I'm home," and
   you are home.

5. Your kids call you on your cell phone to say, "Dad, can
   you pass the salt?"

6. You have to "work up" to opening your cell phone
   bill.

7. You don't care that your headset gives you bad hair.

8. You believe it's okay to call your mom and say, "Happy
   Mother's Day, Mom. Oh, wait a second . . . I'll have a
   double-decaf mocha latte to go."

9. You think the "Can you hear me now?" commercial is
   actually funny.

10. You would still pump your gas and talk on your cell
    phone even if the urban legend that cell phones cause
    gas tanks to explode proved to be true.

THE JERKS CAN—
SO WHY NOT?

A colleague of mine was reflecting about technology and how it's changed our expectations of connecting with others. He said, "Technology, especially cell phones, has changed our connections with others. We expect to be able to reach someone at any time or any place and, as such, being reachable becomes the new norm."

He is right, of course; being reachable is the new norm, for jerks and non-jerks alike. And there are lots of benefits. People can get a hold of us so we can leave our houses without worrying that we're going to miss a call. We can leave work knowing that our office will find us. We can let our kids go out knowing that we can contact them. And, now, we can even take a picture of the sofa we're thinking of buying and call our mom to get a second opinion.

Anybody can reach us and we can call anyone from anywhere. We love the freedom, capability, and convenience. Isn't technology great, and what a time-saver, as any mobile multi-tasker can tell you (and I'm sure they would if they weren't already having two conversations and putting cream in their coffee).

Just Because You Can, Should You?

Yes, technology is great and, yes, we can sometimes save time using a cell phone, but we sometimes take the "can" part too far. Just because you *can* call someone from wherever you may be, *should* you? Just because people *can* reach you, *should* you answer your phone?

The answer is, of course, "no." I'll say that again. The answer is "no."

Non-jerks know this. They take into consideration their environment and realize that their cell phone use may disturb others.

Simply put, the jerks don't. To them, cell phone technology has conveniently and completely removed the boundaries of where you can talk and how many things you can do at once. For the most part, these boundaries are not legal ones, but the social ones that cover how to behave politely and with regard to others in public. To the cell phone jerks, *should* is no longer an issue. You simply *can*.

Cell phone jerks who feel empowered by technology often don't get that for the Rest of Us, the boundaries are not only still there but are being violated by them. In fact, I suspect the jerks are just waiting for the rest of us to catch on to their way of doing things. They probably think we're the old-fashioned ones and they're simply on the cutting edge.

But the Jerks Do Learn

Over time, many of these jerks can, and will, learn or relearn that boundaries do still exist, especially as a result of formal policy restricting cell phone use, including banning them (see the next page) or intervention from the Rest of Us. (See "Know When It's Okay to Do Something," page 145, for specifics.) I have seen some rather amazing transformations happen with some pretty big jerks, so I have hope.

When You Can't, Even Though You Can

Camera phones ... will not be permitted in any press areas at the Seventy-sixth Academy Awards. During the security and screening process, cellular phones and PDAs will be carefully inspected and those with image-capture capabilities will be confiscated.... Cell phones that ring during the interviews with winners will [also] be confiscated.

—Memo sent out by the Academy Awards press office

The camera capability now built-in to many new cell phones is getting them banned from health clubs, classrooms, and social functions. (Word has it that Britney Spears recently banned all cell phones from a party she was throwing because she didn't wanted any unauthorized snapping. Personally, I walk for exercise but if I went to the gym, I would sure feel better knowing there was no picture-taking going on.

Realize That the Jerks Often Don't Know They're Being Jerks

Your next step in your cell phone intervention evolution can be difficult. So here goes. I'm not saying that it's okay or even excusable for the cell phone jerks to behave the way they do, but after working with people for many years I can tell you:

> *Most people—even those obnoxious, loud cell phone jerks—do not set out to intentionally cause difficulty for others.*

Really. As I said earlier, many of the jerks out there just have no idea how their behavior is affecting others. They may be acting rudely by shouting out the details of their sex life on a park bench, but they're usually not cell phone jerks on purpose.

As a business coach, when it comes to jerk-like behavior, I see a lack of self-awareness in people all the time. To the interrupter I'll say, "Do you realize that you just interrupted me again?" To the loud talker I'll say, "Are you aware that you were just shouting again?" These people will seem sincerely shocked and answer, "I had no idea I was even doing that," and I believe them.

In fact, many business professionals—some very high-level ones—who attend my seminars are sent by their bosses to gain an awareness of their own behavior.

I have given hundreds of seminars to thousands of people and no one in any of my seminars has ever been the cause of the difficulty. (Isn't that interesting?) Rude behavior is like any behavior; it becomes a habit. And if no one points out the problem to the jerk, the behavior usually continues.

Aren't you going to feel a little less angry toward someone if you thought they weren't deliberately trying to disturb you? You may still be annoyed but your response is less likely to be rude also. But, if you're convinced that these people are just out to torment you and to ruin the quality of your life, then you're likely to be rude, even very rude, back to a cell phone jerk.

"It's-Not-Me; It's-the-other-Guy" Syndrome

I was walking with my neighbor. We usually do this after dinner for exercise. I'm complaining about a man on my train. I like to finish my work on my ride home. He is talking so loudly I couldn't concentrate. My friend is agreeing and sharing some of her cell phone horror stories. And then it happens. Her cell phone rings and she answers it and proceeds to have a conversation with her friend about their lunch meeting for the next day. We are walking and she's talking to someone else.

Get it? Even though we are unaware of our behavior, it doesn't mean that we don't see the jerk behavior in others. Go figure. It's another evolutionary blip. I call this misperception the "It's not me; it's the other guy" syndrome. An Exxon Mobile 2000 Driver Survey uncovered "courtesy gaps," as much as 57%, with drivers tending to view themselves as friendlier than other drivers on the road. And there sure are courtesy gaps when it come to cell phones.

Here's proof:

In a 2003 Harris Interactive poll of 1200 cell phone users:

> ***** 51 percent said Americans use their cell phones in a "somewhat or very discourteous manner."

Yet:

> ***** 86 percent claimed that they, personally, "rarely or never engage in discourteous phone use."

Furthermore:

✱ 80 percent of respondents think the use of the vibrating ringer makes cell phone use acceptable, at least in some situations and 73 percent believe that letting calls go to voicemail can also improve cell phone rudeness.

Yet:

✱ 50 percent have never set a ringer to silent or vibrate, and 45 percent don't use voicemail.

Do the math. There's a disconnect somewhere. (This disconnect between our behavior and our awareness is the reason I've included the jerk tests throughout this book. You may need to tune in to your own behavior because—gasp—you, too, might be a cell phone jerk—by accident, of course.)

BUT SOME JERKS
REALLY ARE JERKS

Alas, there are some jerks out there that are aware that they are exhibiting bad behavior and just don't give a damn.

True cell phone jerks are similar to the strains of bacteria that are immune to antibiotics. I don't think there are a lot of them, but make no mistake, there's just no getting rid of them.

These jerks are immune to CPEGs. No matter how many times you may say, "Please keep it down," they will ignore you or even give you a nasty reply. During cell phone courtesy month in July, they may even go out of their way to download annoying ringtones, like the theme from *Bonanza* and talk even louder.

The true cell phone jerks of the world feel that because they can, they are entitled to, regardless of how you or I feel about it or its impact upon us.

These are the people who use their cell phones even when the sign says, *"No cell phones please."*

They are the cell phone jerks who refuse to listen, say there is no law against its use, and therefore claim it's their right to use the cell phone whenever and wherever they may choose.

Why do true jerks exist? I don't know. I wish I did.

We could spend hours trying to analyze them, but that is beyond the scope of this book. Maybe Freud could have figured them out. For the Rest of Us, it's just better to learn how to handle them.

When Dealing with a Jerk, Don't Become a Jerk Yourself

[If] you and I were on a cross-country bus, and you decided to make a series of phone calls, I would have to smash it. I wouldn't want to, I would be obliged to, to be ethically consistent.

—RANDY COHEN, *NEW YORK TIMES* COLUMNIST OF "THE ETHICIST"

(I'd hate to think of what he'd want to do if he were the unethicist columnist.)

Yes, the jerks drive us crazy. Yes, it's okay to speak up and PEG a cell phone jerk, but no, it's not okay to become a jerk yourself when you react to a cell phone jerk. (I know you don't want to hear this but I know you know it's true: Someone else's bad behavior is no excuse for your own.) It's not okay to "lose it," even if you feel morally or ethically justified.

Unfortunately, many people do.

WHEN GOOD PEOPLE
ACT LIKE JERKS

That's Life

There are plenty of ordinary instances of ordinarily nice people responding rudely to cell phone jerks. When people act rudely to the jerk, there is often a backlash and sometimes there is a "nolash" (I just made that word up to mean the jerk's cell phone behavior remains unchanged) as the following two stories illustrate.

A friend sheepishly told me this story:

I was at the movies watching the Ya Ya Sisterhood *when the woman in front of me answered her cell phone and started talking on it. I was so angry. I leaned over and wasn't very nice when I said, "Hey, lady, take it outside." She said something back and then I said I was going to get the manager. She con-*

tinued talking and I called her a "bitch," loud enough so she would hear it. At first, I felt very smug and indignant. Then, I started feeling badly about calling her a bitch. Her two young daughters were with her. It was a terrible thing to say.

If I had to do it all over again, I would have said, "Can you please take it outside? I can't hear the movie." If she'd refused then I would have just gotten the manager and kept my mouth shut.

At the time, my friend, who I can assure you is a lovely person, was fueled by anger and a feeling of righteousness as she called the cell phone jerk a "bitch." Why? Because the cell phone jerk was rude. But later, she regretted her reaction. Why? Because she was being a jerk, too.

A British colleague shared this experience:

I was on the train on my way home. There was a woman with a cell phone droning on and on, at the top of her voice, of course. She was quite annoying and there were many of us exchanging those weary looks that cell phone abusers inspire. We could hear the entire conversation. She was planning to have her husband pick her up at a certain stop as they were then going to meet friends for dinner. Except she didn't realize that she had gotten on the express train, not the local. And not one of us told her about it.

At the time, I felt smug about it, that she had gotten

her comeuppance for her rude behavior. Yet when she'd realized what had happened and her stop whooshed by, she became quite distressed.

I then felt like an awful toad. I should have said something. I ended up feeling badly, yet she was the jerk on the cell phone.

Reach Out and Shush Someone

When *Knight Ridder* reporter Bronwyn Lance Chester was at the movies and a woman answered her cell phone and proceeded to talk, he described the shushing syndrome this way:

The shushing that ensued sounded like a den of hissing snakes. She ended her conversation. About an hour later, her phone rang again, and she proceeded to talk once more. We were dumbstruck at her lack of common courtesy . . .

I am also dumbstruck that someone would behave that way in a crowded theater, but the den of hissing snakes is usually not an effective strategy, either. Occasionally it works, but often the cell phone jerk perceives it as a rude attack. I know a lot of people don't want to hear this, but loud shushes, though easy and often anonymous, are by nature, rude. On top of that, as the above story illustrates, it usually doesn't change the jerk's behavior, hence the "nolash."

Recognizing the Jerk Within

You exhibited jerk behavior, if you've ever:

* Done the finger wag in someone's face while saying, "Stop it right there. And do NOT tell me you have the right to use your cell phone right in my face."
* Been invited to appear on the Jerry Springer show to give (nasty) advice on handling cell phone jerks.
* Spoken any louder to the jerk than the jerk on the cell phone was talking.
* Cursed or swore, even if the jerk was cursing and swearing and even if it was only under your breath.
* Required a towel to wipe your face off after confronting a cell phone jerk.
* Thrown popcorn at the back of a cell phone jerk's head, especially if was buttered.
* Said, "I think I speak for all of us . . ." Even though you probably do, you might not, so why make the jerk feel like he or she is about to be throttled by a train full of upset people? One upset person usually is enough to get a jerk's attention.
* If you, along with the cell phone jerk, were "shown" or "thrown" to the door.

Rude Behavior Begets Rude Behavior

Your rude behavior may also bring out even more rude behavior from jerks. The jerks end up being offended and blinded by your rude behavior and they don't recognize that their inappropriate cell phone use may have started the problem, as this story illustrates:

My husband and I were in our local coffee shop. A woman was talking loudly on her cell phone. It was a small, quiet place. She was being disruptive.

After a few minutes, a man who was trying to read, and who was obviously annoyed by her, suddenly belted out, "Hey, lady, shut up! Nobody cares about your stupid life." This woman was clearly shocked and yelled back, "Shut up yourself!" At this point the manager came out and tried to calm things down. But the man just left the coffee shop and the woman, of course, continued her conversation.

Unfortunately, the rude man had no impact upon her. She was too busy dwelling on the fact that he was jerk, which he was, to consider that she might have been a jerk, too. This happens a lot.

The above stories of good people behaving badly against the cell phone jerks unfortunately show us that when you are rude to a cell phone jerk:

➤ You often don't feel good about yourself. Sure, there's that initial high of letting that annoying jerk "have it," but for most of us it doesn't last.

➤ Rude behavior invites rude behavior.

➤ You run the risk of not even affecting the jerk's behavior.

Know When It's Okay to Do Something

You don't have a badge, handcuffs, or even a whistle. You are not, just in case I've given you the wrong impression, the CPEG police.

Having the right to speak up, doesn't mean you go around PEGing all people on all cell phones in all places. You don't want to do a "Blanche" on every person with a phone. Let me explain . . .

Blanche—not her real name—was a woman I met a few weeks ago at a party. When she found out I was writing this book, she practically stalked me and finally cornered me at the buffet table. "Oh, have I got stories for you," she assured me. She told me her "jerk" stories. She had a lot of them; too many, in fact. It quickly became apparent that I wasn't going to be eating anytime soon and that, to Blanche, anyone on a cell phone was a jerk. Here's one of Blanche's stories:

There was a man on a cell phone in the grocery store, standing in front of the canned tomatoes. He said, "Now what kind am I supposed to get?" I think he was talking to his wife via cell.

So I told him, "Ever hear of a shopping list?" and then I walked away. Forget being nicey nice. You have to go right up to them and make them pay attention to you.

I told her I didn't think that was awful, a man calling his wife from the grocery store to ask her a quick question about tomatoes. "Was he shouting?" I asked. "No," said Blanche. "Was he blocking the aisle?" I asked. "No," said Blanche, "but it annoys me to see all of these people on cell phones. I just hate it, don't you? I wish there were police who could arrest these people or at least slap them with some tickets."

If I hadn't been starving, I would have tried to explain to Blanche (politely, of course) that the only time it's appropriate and fair to PEG a person on a cell phone is if they are actually being a jerk.

Let's not kid ourselves or be unrealistic. Cell phones are here to stay and you can't walk up to every person you meet and "Blanche" him or her.

KNOWING WHEN IT IS OKAY TO PEG JERKS

"Before I read about my summer vacation, I'd like to ask that all pagers, beepers, and cell phones be turned off."

Okay, so you're not going to go crazy handing out CPEG cards like they're your business card, but you do need to be clear about when it's okay to say something to a cell phone jerk. Here are questions you should ask yourself before you proceed:

1. Is the person really being a jerk?

Though there are always exceptions, but generally a person on a cell phone is a jerk if he or she is:

> Shouting.
> Using a cell phone when there's a sign nearby that reads, *"No cell phones, please."*
> Interrupting a performance, movie, or a meeting with a ringing cell phone or their conversation.
> Holding up a line or causing you to wait longer because the person is a mobile multi-tasker.
> Having a confidential conversation, which you shouldn't be hearing.
> Taking a picture of something or someone that isn't permitted.

In addition to the above situations, friends, family, and colleagues become jerks when they are:

> Not giving you their full attention because they are answering and talking on their cell phones.
> Driving a car with you as a passenger, but talking on their cell phone to someone else.
> Unaware of their behavior while they are with you. For example, if my husband were to

answer his phone during a concert and have a conversation (which he would never do) I would have to kill him (which I would never do). But I do need to let him know that he's being a jerk because a) maybe he really doesn't know and b) I wouldn't want anyone to think I married a jerk.

2. Is the jerk's behavior just a minor annoyance for you or an ongoing situation?

Is the person shouting on his cell phone passing you in the hallway or sitting next to you for a forty-minute train ride or a dinner out? If it is just a minor annoyance, why not let it go? If you're in for the longer haul, you may want to say something.

3. Are you the right person?

If the jerk's behavior has a direct effect on you, like you're being subjected to shouting, you are often the one to speak up. If the behavior doesn't have an effect on you, i.e., a colleague complaining about someone else's poor cell phone use, you usually would not say anything to the cell phone user, but you could talk to your colleague about how to stop complaining and speak up. In addition, there are often protocols in situations about who speaks up. In business meetings, it is generally the leader of the group or a meeting facilitator. In public places, if the theater or restaurant manager is involved, let the manager do the talking.

4. Is it safe?

If you are ever in an unsafe situation, let it go. Period. I mean it. End of discussion.

Speaking Up to People You Know

My friend Carl is a great person, but he's always on his phone and it's beyond annoying. It's insulting. When we're out to dinner, he spends half of the time talking on the phone to other people. I don't even want to make plans with him anymore. He calls me and I've stopped calling him back so he'll get the hint that I'm annoyed.

Many people aren't comfortable having confrontations with their friends and others they know well. Yet the consequences of not confronting can be great. Everything from lost friendships to feeling bad about yourself may result in you not saying anything. No one is perfect, especially our friends and family. Either accept their poor cell phone use as a quirk of their personality and let it go, or say something.

Choose the Best Way to Respond to the Jerk

n the first part of this book, I've given you what I call polite and powerful suggestions for handling the cell phone jerks. Now, it's time to put them all together. When confronted with a cell phone jerk you have four main options. Here they are:

OPTION

1

SAY SOMETHING.

I'll say it again: Someone else's bad behavior is no excuse for your own. Instead, stick with a simple, polite CPEG line that identifies what you would like the jerk to do. And if you know ahead of time what's an appropriate line to say, you are more comfortable saying it. Here are some sample lines that have worked for me and many other people I've trained:

> *"Excuse me. Could you please lower your voice?"*
> *"Could you please put your phone on vibrate? The ringing is disturbing."*
> *"Would you please lower your voice? I can hear your conversation."*
> *"This is a no cell phone zone. Could you please take your call elsewhere?"*

What these lines have in common:

> They don't try to explain modern civilization. These lines are simple and to the point. There is no editorializing and no critiquing beyond cell phone use. So no, "Please don't let your phone ring and another thing, could you ease up on the perfume? There are people with allergies here."
> They present your request in the form of a question. A question is less direct and less demanding than issuing forth a command like, "Lower your voice . . ." A question gives the impression that the person has a choice. (Which, of course, we hope they don't realize they have a choice.)
> There is no back-paddling, no excuse-giving, or apologizing.

Your CPEG line can be stronger and more direct if you are talking to people who work for you. Here are some examples:

➤ *"Please lower your voice. I can hear your conversation."*
➤ *"Please don't let your phone ring. It's disturbing to others."*
➤ *"Please take your call outside. Your conversation is disturbing the group."*

Sometimes, when you're in charge, you can just use nonverbal signals. I've been in meetings where the person in charge gives the neck-slice gesture that means, "Knock it off and if not, you're gonna get it." This can be viewed as humorous but also aggressive. Though it doesn't happen very often anymore, if someone answers a phone in my seminar, I will usually just point to him or her and then point to the door. Of course, I'm also smiling.

Five Ways to Not Become a Jerk Yourself When Speaking Up

1. Don't "you" the person to death. By that, I mean resist the urge to blame by starting out with "You shouldn't . . ." or "You are rude, though you probably don't realize it . . ." Think about it, when you're in hot water with your significant other and he or she says, "You just . . ." or "You should . . ." or "You can't . . ." don't you think, "Oh, no, I'm in for it." As illustrated in the examples on the previous page, begin your line with the less direct use of "you," such as "would you" or "could you," or the more direct "please."

2. Pay attention to your voice—both tone and volume—when delivering your CPEG. I have a friend who insists he's polite and powerful and he is except for his tone of voice, which always sounds exasperated during a confrontation. If you are shouting or have a harsh or sarcastic tone to your words, like, "Can you *puuuulllleeasseee* lower your voice," the line would be perceived as aggressive.

3. No apologies, please. You have a right to speak up and as long as you're nice about it and reasonable, what do you have to apologize for? (Women do this more than men, but that's a whole other issue.)

4. Don't keep talking about it. This is especially true when you know the person. For example, if you poke

155

your head over your cube and say, "Daryl, I can hear your conversation, can you keep it down, please?" that will do it. You don't need to explain that you are overloaded with deadlines or that you're really tired. Just say what you need to say and then be quiet. (This is going to be a challenge for many of you, but over time, you'll catch on.)

5. No damning facial expressions. If you're doing the Glare of Doom or the Glance with a Thousand Knives at someone, whatever you say isn't going to sink in because it's likely to be perceived as rude or hostile.

It can't be that simple?

"No," you're saying, "you're teasing me. Silencing a cell phone jerk cannot really be this easy."

Many times it is. Silencing a cell phone jerk can really be that simple, especially if you say your line, say it nicely, and then stop talking.

If you were the jerk, wouldn't those lines have an affect on your behavior? Really, wouldn't they? Unless you were raised by wolves, those lines probably would affect you.

Remember: Don't apologize, make excuses, or backtrack when you say something. Just bask in your own polite and powerful glory.

GIVE OUT A CPEG CARD.

I like to think of the CPEG cards as the next best alternate to speaking up. It's a good way to "reach out and
touch someone," without getting too close. Handing the
jerk a card with a polite and powerful CPEG line on it
doesn't interrupt the person's conversation, and for some
shy people, or those new to positive confrontation, may be
easier to do. It also may stop some people from exploding
at the jerk since the card gives them another way to
respond. (See the back of this book for your own cards.)

Even if you don't give out the card, having one with
you, or tucked into a book, can help you remember what
to say when you do speak up. The three in the back of
this book are good general, all-purpose cards.

If you do choose to respond to a cell phone jerk by
PEGing them with a card, you still need to follow the
guidelines above for speaking up—don't hand it out and
say, "Read it and weep, Bud!" or "Do you ever need to read
this." You also don't want to have the look of hatred, dag-
gers of despair, or the squint of a small animal on your face.

Simply smile, hand over the card, and continue what
you are doing. You may also want to say thank you.

You can order CPEG cards that speak to a wide variety
of situations by visiting my website www.jerkwiththe
cellphone.com, or you can make your own using blank

business cards or index cards—just remember to make them legible, don't use the back of your business card because then the jerk can call you, and keep the lines polite and powerful. Here are some ideas:

CPEG Card Sayings:

RESTAURANT:
> Would you please lower your voice? We can hear your whole conversation.
> You may not realize this but this restaurant has a no cell phone policy for this dining room.
> Could you please put your phone on vibrate? The ringing is disturbing our dinner.

TRAIN:
> This is a quiet car. Could you please move to the cell phone car?
> I'm sure you don't realize this, but you're speaking very loudly. Could you please lower your voice?

MORE CREATIVE ALTERNATIVES:
It can be fun to PEG people with a tailor-made card. Yet keep in mind, that as you get more creative and humorous with your cards, you run the risk of someone not getting your humor, perceiving you as hostile, or missing your point altogether. So be aware of those possibilities before you distribute one of these fun cards:

- Make your fellow passengers happy—not by paying for our tickets (though we wouldn't complain), but just by lowering your voice. Thank you!
- You're being PEGed, Sir/Ma'am. It doesn't hurt and it doesn't cost anything. It just means we would appreciate it if you lowered your voice. We can hear your whole conversation.
- Please make the world a happier and slightly quieter place by lowering your voice. Thank you.
- We hug—and occasionally fall in love with—people who don't yell on cell phones.
- We give a discount to people who don't order while on cell phones. And we really appreciate it!
- Cashiers are people, too! We get hurt when you ignore us. Please hang up and pay!
- Please be sensitive to the enormous egos of our actors. They get really upset when people use cell phones during a performance and we're out of tissues.
- Please, can you take your cell phone conversation outside? We haven't been to the movies since the original *Charlie's Angels* was popular and we really want to enjoy the movie.
- If you don't talk on your cell phone anymore, I'll share my popcorn with you.
- Pssst . . . I'm trying to propose to my girlfriend here and your cell phone conversation is spoiling

the mood. Would you mind lowering your voice? (Thanks.)

FOR PEOPLE YOU KNOW:

➤ Please hang up your cell phone and pay attention to me!

➤ Do I need to call you from my cell phone so you'll answer and talk to me?

➤ I was hoping to have dinner with you, not our waiter. Please hang up and talk to me!

➤ Please hang up so we can catch up.

DRIVERS:

I don't recommend giving cards to drivers. It's just too dangerous, even if the car is stopped at a stoplight. I also don't recommend following people to their destinations in order to hand out a card. Not only would this make you a jerk; you'd also qualify as a stalker. But if I could give a driver a card, and there are days that I would really like to, the following are my fantasy lines for drivers:

➤ Call me old-fashioned, but isn't it better to actually drive with your hands on the steering wheel? Why not hang up and drive?

➤ You've been caught DWCP—Driving While Cell Phoning. Haven't you heard? It's not safe.

TAKE A PERSONAL STAND.

As I've already discussed earlier in this book, there are informal and formal policies that many companies, businesses, and state governments are adopting to regulate cell phone use among their employees, customers, and/or general public. If you're in a position to do this as a business manager, owner, or state legislator, that's great—go for it.

Most of us, however, are not in a position to set official policy, but we can take a personal stand. Here are some inspirations:

➤ An executive I know has a policy that he will not discuss business with anyone on a cell phone. He politely and powerfully explains, "There are privacy issues, so we need to conduct our business on a landline."

➤ A mom whose two teenage sons have cell phones, laid down the law, saying, "If you ever talk on a cell phone while driving, or drive in a car with someone on a cell phone, you will not only lose your cell phone privileges, you will lose your driving privileges, too."

➤ A friend refuses to talk to anyone on a cell phone while they're driving. She explains, "I don't want to be on the phone and hear or in any way be party to an accident. That would be horrible."

➤ A man in one of my seminars said that when he goes out to dinner with certain cell phone jerkish friends, he suggests, "It's so hard for us to get together, why don't we all turn off our cell phones and just enjoy each other's company."

➤ My colleague Clare takes this approach, "Whenever one of my friends calls me from a cell phone and I feel like they're not focused on the call, I just speak up and say something like, 'You know, you sound really distracted why don't you call me back later when you're home and can relax.'"

OPTION

4

LET IT GO.

This last suggestion is also important. You may think it is wimpy. It's not. Letting it go means *choosing* not to respond negatively to a jerk. If, for the most part, you're dealing with the cell phone jerks when you can, you won't feel like every cell phone jerk on the face of the Earth is hacking away at your soul with an ice pick.

After a seminar, a woman, who had previously taken my Polite and Powerful Seminar came up to tell me this story:

I used to get so mad at people who drove while talking on cell phones. I would sit in my car and stew about it. But now that I've been practicing the polite and powerful approach as a way to deal with my annoying co-workers, the jerks on the phone don't bother me as much. I think I'm just less angry because I'm dealing with what I can. It's nice not to get mad all the time when I'm driving.

Not only did this make my day, it makes my point. When you take action when it's important or necessary to do so, it really is easier to let things go in other situations. And it's empowering not to feel mad and stressed out by other people's behavior. Try it.

Impolite but, Unfortunately, Powerful options

There are two suggestions that have become popular for dealing with the cell phone jerks, but I don't think they're very effective. Yes, they may occasionally jolt the cell phone jerk and the message may sink in, but they should never be your first line of defense when dealing with a jerk. Why? You guessed it—these actions can often make you a jerk, too.

Putting In Your Two Cents Worth

A friend of mine sometimes adds comments to loud cell phone talkers' conversations, such as, "Well, I agree, I would leave him, too," or "If it makes you feel more attractive, I don't think it's weird to shave the hair on your chest." If the person gets upset and says, "This is a private conversation," she says, "I'm sorry. I didn't realize that. It seemed as if you were including all of us in your conversation."

She doesn't care if it is impolite. She feels powerful because she is speaking up and believes she is getting her message across. But what usually happens is that the jerk just thinks you're nuts or one of those strange people who always goes around putting in their two cents. The jerk is usually left unchanged.

Sarcasm

I don't recommend sarcasm. It's indirect and can be taken as rude. Sarcasm would be saying something like, "Excuse me, could you speak up a little more? My grandmother forgot her hearing aid."

I'm no fan of sarcasm, so I hate to admit this, but sarcasm on rare occasions may just work with a jerk—if, and this is a big if, you pull it off.

Frankly, you need to have a certain personality—a charming and engaging one—in order to be sarcastic without people thinking that you're very immature or nasty. But, you might be perceived as being uncharming, immature, and nasty, anyway. So, don't do this. In fact, forget I even brought it up.

Respond Appropriately to the Response You Get

You decide to speak up to a cell phone jerk. Two things can happen:

1. You do everything right—good word choice, good volume control, even your hair is fabulous. You say your line, "Excuse me. Could you please lower your voice?" You could win the polite and powerful award for cell phone jerk intervention— that's how good you are.

    And it works. The jerk says, "Oh, okay," "Sorry, I didn't know I was shouting," or they just lower their voice or excuse themselves, so you know it worked.

    We love when this happens. And it does happen.

    Now what?

If the reformed jerk is still in your vicinity, you can smile or say, "Thanks," or "I appreciate that." However, don't keep talking about why you asked them to lower their voice, because the next thing you know, you're saying too much and perhaps apologizing, unless of course, he's single and you're single, and sparks—the good kind—fly and then by all means, chat him up.

2. You do everything right—good word choice, good volume control, even your hair is fabulous. You say your line, "Excuse me. Could you please lower your voice?" You could win the polite and powerful award for cell phone jerk intervention—that's how good you are.

Uh-oh. It has worked well in the past, but this time, something different is happening.

The cell phone jerk says, "No, I can't lower my voice," or "I have better idea, why don't you take it outside," or "This is a private conversation." Or, worse, the jerk makes a bogus constitutional claim like, "It's a free country," or some lame retort like that.

We hate when this happens. And it does happen. Now, you're sitting there with that proverbial egg on your face, the color of which probably matches your hot pink ears, and suddenly it all feels wrong, you wish you'd never read this book, and just wait until you get your hands around my neck . . .

THE EIGHTY PERCENT
INTERVENTION FACTOR

Before you strangle me, let me say that the fear of dive-bombing during a cell phone intervention often stops people from speaking up, but it usually doesn't happen.

However, the flip side of "but it usually doesn't" is that it sometimes does. After reading my book *The Power of Positive Confrontation*, a woman commented, "You know Barbara this is a great book, but it will only work 80 percent of the time."

"Well, read it again," I said. "Maybe you'll pick up the missing 20 percent."

(Not really, I'm just reinforcing my point that sarcasm is often a lousy way to communicate.) What I really said was, "You're absolutely right. But don't you think if you can confront someone successfully 80 percent of the time, that's pretty good, especially considering the alternative that nothing will change if you don't try?"

Bombing-out can occur, yet success is more likely.

WHAT TO DO IF YOU ARE REBUFFED

You don't have control of the other person. You only have control over yourself. And if there's ever a time to exert that control it's when you're being rebuffed by a jerk on a cell phone—because your blood will be boiling and only your indignation will be hotter.

This really is the time not to succumb to your basest fantasies concerning cell phone jerks. This is not the time to explode or mumble.

Mumbling, by the way, is never a good idea. It only opens the door to the jerk saying, "What did you say?" and you responding, "I said, 'Even your mother thinks you're ugly!"

The problem with trying to deal with the die-hard, CPEG resistant strains of cell phone jerks that I think of as the strep of the cell world, is that nothing—absolutely nothing—you're going to say, no matter how polite and powerfully you say it, is going to sink in or jolt them into a more courteous reality.

These are the kind of extreme jerks, who when you do engage with them, get you *so* mad you either get aggressive—like in a road rage or cell rage incident—or inspire you to revert to childish behavior. Suddenly you find yourself saying things like, "Oh, yeah . . . well, I'm rubber, you're glue, whatever you say, bounces off of me and sticks to you." Wouldn't that be great if that were true?

But it's not, so focus on your previous successes and try some or all of the following tactics:

1. Acknowledge their reaction and calmly, calmly, calmly restate your position. Use this one cautiously but sometimes clarifying what you said can help. "I wasn't trying to offend you. I'm only asking you to please lower your voice. It's hard to hear the speaker." Or, "I apologize if I offended you. I'm just asking you to lower your voice so I can read my book." Make sure your tone is calm and those thousand knives behind your eyes, stay behind your eyes. If you stay calm, you have a better chance of defusing the jerk.

2. Get the manager if there is one. If there's a cell phone jerk who is ruining your experience and you're someplace like a restaurant or movie theater, don't engage the jerk any further, especially if the jerk turns hostile, but ask the management to intervene. You have to weigh the fact that you might miss part of the show or movie. But if you're going to be distracted by the person anyway, it may be worth dashing out to the lobby and enlisting help.

3. If you feel compelled to engage the jerk further, at least have a good comeback prepared. There is nothing worse than encountering a jerk and then going home and suddenly realizing what you should have said. *Mad Magazine* had a column called "Snappy Comebacks to Stupid Questions," and I use that as my inspiration.

Silly Constitutional Claim: It's my First Amendment right.
Snappy Comeback: Go yell "fire" in a theater and see what happens to you!

Silly Constitutional Claim: It's a free country.
Snappy Comeback: Go yell "fire" in a theater and see what happens to you!

Silly Constitutional Claim: It's not against the law.
Snappy Comeback: Go yell "fire" in a theater and see what happens to you!

Okay, so maybe I'm stretching the concept of "snappy," but when you're an etiquette expert you're limited by niceness. It's not polite to say nasty things. (P.S.: You're really better off skipping this one and going right to number four.)

4. Shrug your shoulders, tell yourself, "I spoke up. I tried. That gets me points." Then go to your imaginary "happy, cell-phone free place." Remember, most people aren't jerks. Of course, the big, neon, blatant jerks are memorable but that doesn't mean there are many of them. Take a deep breath and let this one go. (Try the "Cell Phone Serenity Now Prayer" on the next page; it may give you strength.)

5. Imagine the jerk in his or her underwear. I know, it's the oldest trick in the book, but it must work for some people or, I assume, it wouldn't be in the book at all. Seriously, try to remember that the jerk may not be a jerk all the time, just a person having a bad day. Doesn't that happen to you sometimes?

   You also have to consider the fact that later on, alone in his or her shame, the cell phone jerk may be visited by the ghost of cell phone incidents past and have a revelation: "I was acting like a jerk. Ouch. Maybe I am a jerk." People will change their behavior when they're out of view in order to save face.

The "Cell Phone Serenity Now Prayer"

On the television show *Seinfeld*, George's father used to scream "Serenity Now! Serenity Now!" when he was really upset. Sometimes, when it comes to the cell phone jerks, we need to invoke the "Serenity Now Prayer," take a deep breath, and let our anger and stress go.

Oh Higher Power, grant me the serenity
to accept the cell phone jerks
who never stop talking,
who always have a fresh battery,
who download obnoxious ringtones from the Internet.

Courage to PEG the
cell phone jerks who seem more reasonable
(or at least smaller than me);
and the wisdom to know the difference,
so I don't get punched in the nose
or hurled from a fast-moving train.
Amen.

8

And One More Thing

When it comes to cell phones, let's face it, we have opened Pandora's Box and there's no going back to the simple days of landlines and pay phones. Nor would we want to.

The technology is not only here to stay, it's becoming more and more entrenched in our lives. Not so long ago, futurists predicted that one day we will all carry cell phones that give us the capability not only to call people, e-mail, and surf the web, but also do our banking and provide directions. The future has arrived, in Japan anyway, but the Rest of Us aren't far behind. Believe it or not, there are even scientists and engineers out there working on imbedding a birth-control device into cell phones, and I saw an ad online the other day that uses the cell phone to help people stop snoring. (Can "Beam me up, Scotty" be far behind?) But just because cell phones are a fact of life or the realization of a technological society, doesn't mean they have to drive us crazy. We can use our phones responsibly (which I'm sure you do) *and* we can practice the steps I've given you with the cell phone jerks when they don't.

I've given you a polite and powerful approach that allows you to confront the jerk with success—maybe not all of the time, but a lot of the time. But you don't have to run out and try all of my suggestions at once. Take it slowly. Pick the ones that are important to you. Let the ones go that aren't. Build your confidence. Enjoy your successes.

Let me leave you with one final thought. Remember, if you're not part of the cell phone solution, at least you can tell me a good story about a cell phone jerk. Just like reformed cell phone jerks, the world always has room for more good cell phone jerk horror story and I'm just the person to tell it to. You can send your stories to me via the contact information on the following page.

Acknowledgments

Everyone always says, "This book would never have been written without . . ." but we really mean it. This book would not have come into the world without our publisher Matthew Lore. This book was his brainchild. Without his passion and commitment to inspire a new and improved world of cell phone users, this book would have gone unwritten.

Though *The Jerk with the Cell Phone* was his idea, he was completely generous with our vision for it. He trusted us to do the job and for that we are truly grateful.

We also want to thank Peter Jacoby, Matthew's assistant, for all his support and hard work in fine-tuning the manuscript. Further thanks goes to designer Pauline Neuwirth, whose inspired design captures the spirit and sensiblity of this work.

B.P. and S.M.

About the Authors

Barbara Pachter is a business communications consultant, coach, and seminar leader who speaks nationally and internationally on topics including assertiveness, business etiquette, international communications, conflict, women's issues, and presentation skills. She has conducted over 1,500 skill-building seminars for clients including DaimlerChrysler, Merck & Co., NASA, and Pfizer, Inc. She is the co-author of six books on business etiquette and communication skills, including *The Prentice-Hall Complete Business Etiquette Handbook*, *The Power of Positive Confrontation*, and *When the Little Things Count . . . And They Always Count.* She lives in Cherry Hill, New Jersey.

Susan Magee, an award-winning writer, is the author of the humorous travel guide *UFO USA* and co-author of several other books, including *Why Can't You Read My*

Mind and, with Barbara Pachter, *When the Little Things Count* and *The Power of Positive Confrontation*. She lives with her family outside of Philadelphia, Pennsylvania.

☛

Barbara Pachter can be reached at:

Pachter & Associates
P.O. Box 3680
Cherry Hill, NJ 08034
Telephone: 856.751.6141
Fax: 856.751.6857
E-mail: pachter@comcast.net
Web: www.pachter.com
www.jerkwiththecellphone.com